Soupy Sal
Detroit Experience

MW01484208

Soupy Sales and the Detroit Experience:

Manufacturing a Television Personality

By

Francis Shor

Cambridge
Scholars
Publishing

Soupy Sales and the Detroit Experience:
Manufacturing a Television Personality

By Francis Shor

This book first published 2021. The present binding first published 2021.

Cambridge Scholars Publishing

Lady Stephenson Library, Newcastle upon Tyne, NE6 2PA, UK

British Library Cataloguing in Publication Data
A catalogue record for this book is available from the British Library

ISBN (10): 1-5275-7640-X
ISBN (13): 978-1-5275-7640-7

PRAISE FOR THE BOOK

"Francis Shor has done the painstaking research of relating Sales' evening program, "Soupy's On," to the jazz life of Detroit. Many prominent jazz artists appeared on the program when they played in Detroit jazz clubs. This is a most unique and valuable addition to Detroit jazz history."
—Lars Bjorn
Professor Emeritus of Sociology, University of Michigan; author (with Jim Gallert), *Before Motown: A History of Jazz in Detroit*

"An entertaining read about a beloved pop-cultural icon that also captures the complexity of Detroit's economic, political, and social landscape in the 1950s. This book will change the way you understand Soupy Sales's humor, the wild popularity of his TV show, and his enduring impact on an entire generation of viewers. This is cultural history with pie-in-the-face explanatory power."
—Catherine Cangany, PhD
Executive Director, Jewish Historical Society of Michigan; author, *Frontier Seaport: Detroit's Transformation into an Atlantic Entrepôt*

"Mention the name Soupy Sales to any Baby Boomer and you'll most likely be met with a huge smile and a memory of one of his whacky shows that appealed as much to adults as they did to children. But few know about the early days in Soupy's career, and the soil into which the seeds of his comic sensibilities were planted. Francis Shor does a terrific job of chronicling Soupy's early days in television, especially those important Detroit years, before he made it to Los Angeles and then New York, where he created some of his most memorable characters. Shor makes a compelling case for placing Sales squarely in the pantheon of other legendary TV comedians like Pinky Lee and Milton Berle."
—Charles Salzberg
Co-Author (with Soupy Sales), *Soupy Sez: My Life and Zany Times* and twice-nominated Shamus Award author of the Henry Swann series

CONTENTS

ACKNOWLEDGEMENTS

The inspiration for writing this book can be traced to a number of sources, not the least of which was the desire to be distracted from the perilous times in which we live. Other motivating factors may be more difficult to discern. However, between the inspiration for and execution of the manuscript, there are conspicuous contributions that I need to acknowledge.

First of all, there were several individuals who graciously shared their knowledge of Soupy Sales from their own prior work on his life and times. Both Ed Golick and Charles Salzberg relayed information and read certain sections of the manuscript, providing invaluable feedback. Kathy O'Connell was not only a ready source of previously unpublished material and memorabilia about Soupy, but also a constant cheerleader for my project. Janet Oseroff helped make important connections to a variety of sources.

Secondly, I was able to interview a number of people closely connected to Soupy's television shows. Jane Adler (Clyde's widow), Joe Messina (guitarist for Soupy's house band), and Leon Weiss (son of Rube Weiss, co-star of *Soupy's On* sketch comedy routines) freely provided precious recollections of their various interactions with Soupy.

For feedback on specific chapters and overall technical help, I want to thank three former colleagues, Lisa Alexander, Tom Klug, and Marie Sweetman.

I also want to acknowledge those interviewees who were, in most cases, first contacted by email. After completing a questionnaire that I generated concerning past social and personal situations related to living in Detroit and watching Soupy's shows, I followed up, in several instances, with telephone conversations about those matters. Although some of those interviewees requested anonymity, I want to thank the following for their contributions to my research and writing of this book: Ricky Stoler, Suzanne Lareau, Tom Fleisher, Bill Harris, Frank Joyce, Rick Kotlarz, Joanne Kristal, Suzanne Harris Paul, Natan Fuchs, Jeffrey Weiss, Mike Harrison, Marc Nowakowski, Sarah Morgenstern, Cheryl Brent Erickson, Barry Grant, Barry Hoffman, and Ralph Franklin.

Ralph Franklin, along with several other close friends, Chris Collins, Bill Meyer, Rudy Simons, Peter and Marilyn Werbe, regaled me with their own memories of growing up in the Detroit area. In the process, they aided me in innumerable ways in identifying Soupy's impact and the lay of the cultural landscape in the Motor City during the 1950s. Ralph also provided invaluable technical assistance.

Finally, as always, my family offered loving support and sustenance. My wife, Barbara Logan, has been an incredibly giving partner in life, even in the face of my irascible moods at times. My amazing adult children, Molly, Miriam, and Finn, have been stalwart sustainers for almost all of my endeavors. My grandkids, Ruby and Iris, are continuing delights for whom I gladly dispense my *zayde* zaniness.

While I was completing the first draft of the manuscript, my 100 year-old father, Martin Shor, passed away. I dedicate this book to his memory.

INTRODUCTION

On a certain Saturday morning in the fall of 1959 I happened to be home in the suburban community just outside Pittsburgh where our family resided. Apparently, my junior high football team, to which I belonged as a first-string defensive back and second-string receiver, did not have a game. There must not have been any other outdoor activities with friends that required my participation that morning. So, with nothing much to do beyond a few chores, I gravitated to the living room and turned on the television set. The TV was situated in a strategic corner that could be seen from all points in the living room and even from the steps that led up to the second story bedrooms. I would often sneak down these stairs, hidden from my parents' view, to watch those programs that were broadcast past my bedtime, like *The Tonight Show*, first with Steve Allen and then Jack Paar, until my brother would call downstairs to my parents, alerting them to my skulking TV transgressions.

As the noon hour approached on this particular Saturday, I switched the channel to the local ABC affiliate. I'm not sure if I was previously alerted to what was scheduled for that time or it was just the serendipity of random selection. However, when *Lunch with Soupy Sales* began with a crazy sounding piano, followed by a guy wearing a big floppy bowtie and a slightly skewed top hat, I was riveted. What flashed before my eyes for the next nearly thirty minutes was a procession of slapstick bits that were not only funny, but also, given my own teenage goofiness, strangely *simpatico* and maybe, dare I say, subversive from a cultural if not political perspective.

Among those silly but mesmerizing acts performed was a bizarrely engaging exchange between this Soupy guy and a creature represented by a woolly white paw that he called "White Fang," aka "the meanest dog in the world." The incongruity of a dog of that stature with one appendage waving back and forth while the attached voice from off camera made noises sounding like "LoLoLo!" was absolutely and hysterically humorous. Added to the mayhem that transpired between this "White Fang" and Soupy were several interruptions from a next-door neighbor knocking on the makeshift door of this rickety-looking set. Again, only a hand was visible while the angry fellow ranted about something and then threw a pie in poor Soupy's face.

It seemed that this bedlam began to subside when Soupy sat down at a lunch table decked out with food items like a grilled cheese sandwich, some potato chips, a glass of milk, and a molded Jell-O desert. As Soupy prepared to consume each and every part of the midday meal, a sound effect would accompany its ingestion. For milk, there was a "mooing" sound and for the Jell-O, an inexplicable "boinging" noise would come with the wiggling plated gelatin that Soupy shook in a close-up for the camera. Advising his youthful audience to have our lunch with him, Soupy's invitation seemed as genuine as the endless commercials for Jell-O seemed a little artificial, as artificial as the food coloring that gave the gelatin a glowing translucent look. Throughout the show Soupy promoted Jell-O and implored his young viewers to beseech their mothers to purchase said item next time she went to the grocery store.

While I could neglect these entreaties for enlisting my Mom to buy Jell-O, especially since she worked and I ate my fill of Jell-O deserts at the prepared school lunches, I was particularly fascinated and amused by the use of silent films during the program. Most intriguing, beyond the novelty of these old time movies, was Soupy's narration which relied heavily on wordplay. The puns that punctuated the characters and plot of these slapstick films endeared me entirely to Soupy's humor. I can still recall one of those funny lines he uttered in his voice-over. As a Model T automobile struggled without much success to negotiate a hill, he commented jocularly: "There goes a Rolls-Knardley. Rolls down one hill and can hardly make it up the next."

I couldn't wait to share what I saw and heard that Saturday on Monday morning with my buddies at school. A few of them had also watched the program and we immediately bonded by repeating some of the lines from Soupy's narration and parts of the routines that we found particularly hilarious. We also established what would become a kind of secret code among us faithful viewers. To the bemusement or disgust of the unknowing others in our junior high hallways, we would often call out to each other with the White Fang voice, "LoLoLo," while flailing our right arm in demonstrable ways that only we, the initiated in Soupy Sales *shticks*, would fully comprehend.

Although the previous reminiscences of *Lunch with Soupy Sales* are tinged with nostalgia, this book is not intended as a breezy fan catalogue of Soupy's shows, especially since practically all the videos or kinescopes of those shows from the 1950s were destroyed. While I do not propose to diminish the importance of audience reception, including my own, such viewership needs to be put in the context of those critical perspectives provided by cultural and media studies. As will be seen initially in the chapter outlines below and then throughout each of the specific individual chapters, these perspectives will inform the subject areas covered in this book that include memory, child development, broadcasting history, Cold War and consumerist ideology, television programming, comedy, Jewish humor and comics, jazz, and Detroit socio-cultural history during the 1950s. All of these seemingly disparate topics, however, lead back to identifying the manufacturing of a television personality at a particular moment in time and in a specific location. Soupy Sales, thus, becomes a figure who reflects the socio-economic, ideological, and cultural meanings of a television personality refracted through the Detroit experience in the 1950s.

Such a critical examination of this particular television personality is not intended to detract from or minimize the humor and entertainment ethos embedded in Soupy's shows. Hopefully, this book can negotiate those hazardous, but essential, theoretical and methodological approaches and the attendant language without sacrificing the pleasures elicited in following Soupy Sales in his entertaining Motor City journeys in the 1950s.

Chapter One, "Manufacturing 'Soupy Sales'," attempts to reconstruct a historical narrative of the television personality who would become "Soupy Sales" at the age of twenty-seven when he began working in 1953 on WXYZ-TV in Detroit. Assessing his memoir, co-authored by Charles Salzberg, and other recollections that can be found in print and on video through the lens of memory studies will provide a necessary opportunity to explore the social and cultural conditions that shaped Soupy from his birth up until he arrived in the Motor City. Reviewing those biographical influences that informed his life story will help locate his public persona as an entertainer, as well as taking account of historical context within which Soupy emerged.

The manufacturing of "Soupy Sales" cannot be separated from the medium that gave him a prominence in popular culture and produced a fan base, especially among kids during those early years of 1950s television. As a developing technology and business institution founded on commercial values, television will be the focus on Chapter Two, "TV and Popular Culture in the 1950s." Television both reflected and refracted popular culture, creating in the process programs that attracted audiences who, in turn, incorporated and transformed the meanings embedded in those shows for their own lives. The critical insights gleaned from the works on television, media, and popular culture studies will be deployed in order to illuminate those social and cultural connotations of 1950s television.

When my friends and I re-enacted the comedic routines we saw on Soupy's lunchtime program, we were not only manifesting our pleasure in what we viewed, but also refracting the various meanings that television and popular culture provided. Understanding the attraction to and re-enactment of this style of comedy, from slapstick to wordplay, with its ties to Jewish television jesters like Milton Berle and Sid Caesar, will be a critical part of this chapter, particularly because of the kinds of humor and comedy *shticks* that regaled audiences on the Berle and Caesar television shows and inspired Soupy in a variety of ways. Accounting for those comedic influences on Soupy and his humor will incorporate those studies of Jewish comedians and comedy by such scholars as Arthur Asa Berger, Lawrence J. Epstein, and Ruth Wisse, among others.

Although we might have been oblivious to deeper social influences of the surrounding culture, Chapter Two will investigate those structural influences that fashioned family life along class and gender lines, especially in the domesticated Cold War and consumerist environment of the times. The conclusion of this chapter will focus on one of the most watched television program for kids of the 1950s – the *Mickey Mouse Club*. What values permeated that program and its contrast to Soupy's style will be highlighted.

Chapter Three, "The Detroit Experience in the 1950s," will consider the political and popular culture contexts within which Soupy's 1953-1960 television programs were situated. Beyond the somewhat insular world of television programming and against its deliberate neglect of the larger economic, political and social forces driving conditions in the Motor City, this chapter will provide a more inclusive sense of what was happening in Detroit during this time period. While Soupy viewed Detroit as his "Mecca" for giving him a television platform from which he gained an incredible following, for others, especially African Americans, the 1950s in Detroit were fraught with racial tensions and persistent discrimination in employment, housing, and criminal justice. Utilizing the studies of Detroit in the 1950s by Daniel Clark, Thomas Sugrue, Heather Ann Thompson, and other urban and social historians should help to give a more critical and enlarged context for what constituted multiple and different experiences. In particular, as the manufacturing hub of the nation in the 1950s, the production of television programming and TV personalities reflected and refracted the contradictory social forces at play in Detroit.

This chapter will also consider those who, like Soupy, arrived to Detroit in the 1950s, bringing with them a different life story and alternative trajectory. The biographies and autobiographies of people like Grace Lee Boggs, a political activist of the left who entered the Detroit scene the same year as Soupy, and Arthur Johnson, the newly appointed Director of the Detroit branch of the NAACP, the largest branch in the country, will offer a better understanding of the complexities and contradictions inherent in the Motor City experience. The insecurities of autoworkers in the erratic employment situation of the Big Three during the 1950s, especially as those corporations began their long march to the suburbs and beyond, will afford the necessary counterpoint to Soupy's rise to prominence and the economic benefits that he accrued with his growing popularity. Also, because Soupy relied on showcasing jazz and popular musicians on his evening program, *Soupy's On* (discussed in much more detail in Chapter Five), the jazz scene, in particular, covered so extensively in Lars Bjorn's *Before Motown* and in part of Mark Stryker's *Jazz from Detroit*, will play a significant role in filling out the political, social, and cultural landscape of the Detroit experience in the 1950s.

During his time on WXYZ-TV, Soupy had a variety of daytime shows that spanned the early morning hours to the noon hour to the early evening. That early evening time slot turned out to be an ABC syndicated summer replacement for the *Kukla, Fran, and Ollie* show during July and August in 1955. The *Lunch with Soupy Sales* ran for a year and a half on ABC television with the final three months of the broadcast coming from Los Angeles. Unfortunately, there are only a few remaining tapes of any of those shows that have been posted publically on either YouTube or other websites. Those scarce postings, nonetheless, will allow for extensive analysis of their content. Additionally, his memoirs, the entry in *TV Land Detroit*, and other archival sources provide both contemporaneous and retrospective commentary. To supplement this material I have extracted relevant material from two-dozen Detroit area residents who responded to my questionnaire about their recollections of his shows and related matter. Finally, archival entries from newspapers of the time, especially the *Detroit Free Press*, will form a significant segment of Chapter Four, "Soupy's Daytime TV Shows."

Chapter Five, "Soupy's Evening TV Program," focuses on the 11 P.M. WXYZ-TV program called, *Soupy's On*. As with the daytime shows, there is a dearth of visual material from either the fifteen minute or thirty minute versions. A few snippets of jazz performances can be found on various websites. Among these are two songs by legendary trumpeter Clifford Brown a few months before his fatal car accident on June 26, 1956 (the only taped appearance of Brown that's known to exist which also became part of the Ken Burns PBS series on *Jazz*) and Erroll Garner shortly after the release of his phenomenally successful 1955 jazz album, *Concert by the Sea*. However, by searching through the TV listings in the *Detroit Free Press* and cross-checking these with local appearances by nationally famous jazz artists performing in Motor City jazz venues, this chapter will reconstruct the musical content of *Soupy's On* and the amazing cavalcade of musicians who performed on that evening show.

Supplementing the account of the musicians and sketch comedy routines on *Soupy's On* will be eyewitness reports of what transpired, several interviews of those connected to the show, and a review of some of the scripts from the comic routines. Among those interviews are the lively reflections by guitarist Joe Messina concerning a number of jazz performers on the show. Joe played in the resident Hal Gordon band on Soupy's evening program and would later achieve his own distinction as a member of the celebrated "Funk Brothers" of Motown fame. Finally, the discussion of Soupy's skits for his evening show will rely on archival material, published commentary by those involved, and interviews with relatives of those who helped to create and perform in those sketches.

Soupy and his producers aggressively marketed his shows, as evident in ads and stories on the TV and other pages of the *Detroit Free Press*. In addition, he kept up a frenetic pace of public appearances from Jewish War Veterans events to emceeing jazz concerts to the Saturday morning promotion of his fan clubs, the Birdbaths, at local Detroit movie theatres. Tracking these myriad public presentations will be the primary subject matter in Chapter Six, "Public Persona and Private Life." Beyond identifying his role in shaping his public persona, this chapter will probe the ways that the public consumed his television personality and the way his career intruded on his private life. The reconstruction of all of these events should also help explain how he achieved such prominence and became one of the most popular television personalities and an entertainment celebrity in the Motor City. As an entertainment celebrity, Soupy Sales "promises to help us comprehend celebrity as a general cultural phenomena: its peculiar dynamics, its place in everyday lives, (and) its broader implications" (Gamson 1994: 3). As we will see in this chapter, that entertainment celebrity status was achieved by the manufacturing of Soupy's television personality built on "promotion, publicity, and performance" (Bennett 2011: 18).

Chapter Seven, "Detroit Afterimages," briefly recounts Soupy's television career after he left Detroit. After a short time in Los Angeles from 1961-1962, he wound up in New York where his 1964-1966 ABC program, *The Soupy Sales Show,* had national syndication. He also did a variety of television turns on syndicated shows that spanned the late 1960s and 1970s, like *What's My Line,* and into the early 1980s with *Sha Na Na.* He returned periodically to Detroit to perform at annual telethons and at a variety of clubs where an early image of innocent child-like behavior morphed into a stand-up comic whose jokes relied on more adult content.

The "Conclusion" will attempt to assess the legacy that remains so much a part of 1950s television and popular culture in the Motor City. The fond memories that many Detroiters retain of Soupy Sales' time in Detroit are not only a testament to his impact, but also to the ways a past, formed in childhood by television and popular culture, continues to resonate in the lives of so many older adults. Apparently, given the number of websites now incorporating his shows, Soupy still manages to attract a passionate following, one that deserves the kind of affectionately critical examination that this book, hopefully, represents.

Finally, in order to pay homage to the kind of jokes that Soupy told and humor he performed, there will be a number of gags and funny stories sprinkled throughout the text. In that regard, let me conclude this introduction with a gag that Soupy included in his compilation of jokes and funny stories, called *Stop Me If You've Heard It!*

Two goats are busy eating garbage. While they're eating, one of them finds a roll of old film and proceeds to eat it up. After he finishes chewing up the film, the other goat asks him, "Did you enjoy the film?"

And the other goat says, "Actually, I preferred the book!" (Sales 2003: 153)

I realize there is no way that this book can match Soupy's ebullience and zaniness on film. However, here's hoping that this book may be a tasty read and provide sustenance for those who are interested in better comprehending the life and times of Soupy Sales, especially during those seven seminal years in Detroit when he became one of the Motor City's pre-eminent television personalities.

CHAPTER ONE

MANUFACTURING "SOUPY SALES"

Born on January 8, 1926 in Franklinton, North Carolina to Irving and Sadie Berman Supman, Milton Supman would begin his twenty-seven year journey to becoming Soupy Sales. That manufacturing of a television and public persona known as "Soupy Sales" would happen in 1953 shortly after his arrival in Detroit. (The name would remain with him until his death in New York City on October 22, 2009.) Indeed, Soupy Sales was, in certain respects, as much a manufactured product as any other that rolled off the assembly line throughout the Motor City, albeit less mechanical and standardized and more organic and idiosyncratic. In effect, Soupy's experiences prior to Detroit equipped him with a self-inventing agency that would serve as a platform for the manufacturing of a television personality par excellence. However, the selling of Soupy Sales as a television personality required endearing himself to an audience and creating a fan base that relied not only on his TV persona but also relentless efforts to be part of the cultural life of Detroit. Tracing the physical and psychological passages traversed by Milton Supman in becoming Soupy Sales will help locate the biographical content and historical and social contexts for that pre-figuring journey to Detroit.

The physical passage is, perhaps, easier to demarcate than the psychological one. Leaving his birthplace in North Carolina after the death of his father in 1931 and remarriage of his mother in 1934, Milton accompanied her and his new stepfather, Felix Goldstein, to Huntington, West Virginia. Graduating high school in Huntington, he would enlist in the navy in 1943 when he was seventeen. Much like millions of other young men during World War II, his service uprooted him from his small-town background and opened up a wider world, punctuated by the terrors of the war in the Pacific. Returning to Huntington after the war, he took advantage of the G. I. Bill to continue his education at Marshall College (now University) in Huntington. From Huntington, he pursued a career in radio and television that took him first to Cincinnati from 1950-1951 and then Cleveland from 1951-1953 before landing in Detroit in 1953 to emerge as the television personality known as "Soupy Sales."

However, it is the psychological passages he navigated in becoming that public persona which provide intriguing insights into the first twenty-seven years of the Soupy Sales life story. As noted by the author of "The Psychology of Life Stories," they "are based on biographical facts, but they go considerably beyond the facts as people selectively appropriate aspects of their experience and imaginatively construe both the past and future to construct stories that make sense to them and to their audiences" (McAdams 2001: 101). For Soupy, in particular, the re-telling of his life story was more than an effort to "interpret certain memories as self-defining" (McAdams 2001: 110). He deployed some of those memories, including manufactured ones, specifically to entertain and impress his audience.

Memories, as innumerable social psychologists and cognitive scientists have confirmed, are fallible. Indeed, the well-known neurologist and author, Oliver Sacks, contends that our "earliest memories, in particular, are susceptible to 'transference' from what one actually experienced to something profoundly significant but without any experiential foundation" (Sacks 2017: 105). This is especially relevant in tracking the earliest memories of the young Milton Supman in North Carolina and discerning the difference between what Sacks calls "narrative truth" as opposed to "historical truth" (Sacks 2017: 119).

In trying to decipher the distinctions between the narrative and historical truths of Soupy's life stories of his earliest memories, I will be relying on the memoir, *Soupy Sez: My Life and Zany Times* (2001), co-authored by Charles Salzberg. (All further page citations will be from this text.) Many of these stories are replicated, like rehearsed scripts, in other published and taped interviews with Soupy. As Salzberg told me in an email exchange concerning the process of constructing Soupy's memoir, his debilitated condition and evident physical impairments at the age of seventy-four when the memoir was written required prompting during Salzberg's interviews with Soupy and filling in any gaps with interviews with friends and family. Even in the absence of a diagnosis of any cognitive problem that may have afflicted Soupy at the time, it is evident that the normal functioning of memory produces distortions, pseudo-reminiscences, and confabulations (Schacter, *et. al.* 2011 and Schnider 2018). My intention in attempting to establish the historical truth underlying any of the distortions and confabulations in Soupy's memoir is not to challenge the authenticity of his narrative truth; rather, it is to provide a more complete historical, social, and cultural context within which his life stories resonate.

Before examining some of those earliest life stories recounted by Soupy, it seems appropriate, if not a little disconcerting, to interject a related joke about memory, one that honors the comedic sensibility that informed his memoirs and his life.

> *A hyena is drinking at the watering hole one day when he sees an elephant approaching for a drink. Close to the water, the elephant stops short and inspects a turtle for a few seconds. Then the elephant rears back and kicks the turtle, making it fly the better part of a mile.*
>
> *The hyena asks, "What did you do that for?"*
>
> *"Well," answers the pachyderm, "About seventy years ago that turtle bit my foot. Today, I finally found that SOB and paid him back."*
>
> *"Seventy years! How in the name of heaven could you remember what it looked like after that many years?"*
>
> *The elephant replied: "I have turtle recall!"* (adapted from Sales 2003: 160)

In looking back at those early years of his life, Soupy obviously could not even approximate total recall. He could and did, however, lace his recollections with jokes and what I would call comedic confabulations. Such comedic confabulations were efforts to translate mundane or traumatic biographical moments into amusing vignettes that deliberately distorted those moments in order to get a laugh from his audience. In effect, Soupy's comedic confabulations became a self-manufacturing process for humorous purposes. As he jokingly recounts, his birth in Franklinton, North Carolina was "primarily because I wanted to be near my mother" (13). This was also probably true for his older brothers, Leonard, born in 1918 and Jack born in 1920. Another brother born in 1916 died the same year Jack was born. According to Soupy, all the living brothers were given nicknames. For Leonard it was "Hambone" (oy, hardly kosher!), for Jack it was "Chickenbone" (14), and for Soupy, the leftover seemed to be "Soupman," eventually to become "Soupy." Actually, it wasn't until his entrance into the media world after leaving Franklinton and Huntington that he would become "Soupy." Prior to this time, he was nicknamed "Suppy" Supman.

While Soupy kidded about wanting "to be near his mother" for his birth, he reveals nothing about her background or his father's in his memoir. A limited online search in a few genealogy sites revealed the bare outlines of the family background. His father was born in Hungary in 1890 and came to the United States with his family. His mother was apparently born in Baltimore in 1897 to Etta and Max Berman, both Jewish immigrants from Russia who were part of he massive wave of Jewish immigration to the United States in the late 19th and early 20th centuries that also brought the Supman family to the country. His mother and father met and married in Baltimore, but moved to North Carolina after World War I, following Irving's brother for a better economic opportunity. When Irving died on September 23, 1931 at the age of forty-one, his body was returned to Baltimore and buried at the B'nai Israel Congregation Cemetery.

Irving and Sadie Supman settled in the small town of Franklinton with a population somewhere between 1200 and 1500 with nary another Jewish family or person in sight. The business they established was a dry goods store they called the "Wonder Department Store." If you're wondering why this Jewish couple would move to a remote part of North Carolina to begin a dry goods business, Soupy doesn't supply an answer. He does, however, offer some jocular cultural commentary from his retrospective comedic lens by noting "if it weren't for bowling, Franklinton wouldn't have any culture at all" (14) and "the main street ran through a car wash" (19).

But it was the pervasive prejudice that animates the recollections of his time in North Carolina in Soupy's memoir, linking it to his later reading of *To Kill a Mockingbird* and his identification with the kids in that novel. Although recounting the grim racist environment of this period, Soupy, nonetheless, constructs a comedic confabulation of his life story to mitigate the prejudice he and his family may have encountered. Joking that his parents sold the Ku Klux Klan its sheets (15), Soupy returns again and again to this comedic confabulation throughout his life, including what can be seen on YouTube in his interview with the fellow comedian, Robert Klein. Stretching even the meaning of narrative truth, Soupy's references to the KKK also contradict many of the historical truths we know about the resurgence of the KKK after WWI and through the early to mid-1920s (MacLean 1994 and Gordon 2017).

The so-called Second Coming of the KKK in the 1920s was not just limited to the South. Outside the South, the KKK exerted tremendous political and cultural influence in Mid-western states, like Indiana,

Western states, like Colorado and Oregon, and cities throughout those regions. In Detroit there were massive rallies of tens of thousands of KKK members whose contender for mayor in 1924 momentarily won the election as a write-in candidate before losing in a recount. Coinciding with renewed white supremacy, xenophobia, and anti-Semitism, the latter particularly pernicious in creating the social-psychological conditions experienced emotionally by the young Soupy, the KKK actually exhausted its dominant influence outside the South by the time Milton Supman was born in 1926. Even in North Carolina, there were no evident chapters of the KKK in Franklinton. This did not, however, diminish the racist and anti-Semitic atmosphere surrounding him and his family.

In particular and at variance with Soupy's comedic confabulation about his family selling the KKK its sheets, Jews were particular targets of the KKK (Gordon 2017: 49-54) and other anti-Semites like Henry Ford and his notorious Michigan-based newspaper, *The Dearborn Independent*. According to historian Linda Gordon, "Jews functioned in Klan discourse to resolve contradictory attitudes towards capitalism and commercialism - by projecting lust for money onto 'the Jew,' Klansmen could adjudge their own profit-seeking as honorable" (Gordon 2017: 61). This profit seeking included the manufacturing of their Klan costumes. KKK members were required to purchase their outfits through the organization (Gordon 2017: 66). So, Soupy's obvious attempt at comedy when it came to the KKK and his family was one of those manufactured confabulations that relied upon the incongruity factor (an essential element of humor as we will see in later chapters) while relieving, perhaps, some painful memories from his childhood.

One of those memories related in *Soupy Sez* was a lynching of a Black man by the KKK. The story that Soupy recounts details the fight between the manager of the local movie theater and a Black patron. From Soupy's retelling of the incident a "violent altercation" occurred when the manager, Mr. Brown, a neighbor of the Supmans, attempted to eject the man for smoking in the area that comprised the segregated section of the theatre, namely the balcony. In the ensuing altercation the manager was thrown to his death. Although the alleged perpetrator was arrested, the KKK snatched him and lynched him from a telephone pole in the center of town. According to Soupy, "This gruesome spectacle left an indelible impression on me. I can still see that man swinging from that telephone pole with the cigarette butt dangling from his mouth, as vividly as if it all happened just last week" (15).

While there may have been an actual lynching that the young Milton Supman observed in Franklinton, North Carolina, there is no evidence from the historical record that this or any such lynching incident took place when Soupy was a child there. In fact, it appears that Soupy was mistakenly mixing up in his memory a similar event that happened in Franklinton in 1919 – seven years before Soupy was born. Some of the details of that incident conform to those presented in Soupy's account. There was a Mr. Brown who was the manager of the Franklinton movie theater. Brown did get into an argument with a Black patron, Powell Green. What transpired next, according to the historical record, was that Brown called the police to arrest Green. As the police tried to lead Green to prison, Brown physically attacked Green. Trying to protect himself, Green managed to wrest a gun from his coat whereupon he shot and killed Brown. As an angry mob formed, police attempted to spirit Green out of town, only to be blocked by a car on the outskirts of the city. The men inside that car exited their automobile and caught Green as he endeavored to escape. They affixed a rope around his neck and dragged him behind the car after which they hung him from a tree (Newkirk 2008: 39-40).

What Soupy appears to exhibit in his own compelling recollection of this story is a kind of false memory, manufactured from those areas of the brain that make it difficult to distinguish actual experiences from imagined ones (Schacter *et. al.* 2011). Given the connections Soupy is making to the emotional horrors of prejudice in his childhood, it is not surprising that a certain manufactured memory becomes part of his reconstruction and re-imagining of the past. As Sacks contends, "Once such a story or memory is constructed, accompanied by a vivid sensory image and strong emotion, there may be no inner, psychological way of distinguishing true from false, nor any outer, neurological way" (Sacks 2017: 120).

Nevertheless, the very real memory of his father's death at the age of forty-one by tuberculosis when Soupy was only five becomes an instance to acknowledge the impact of that loss. As he attests, "His death affected me very much, because after that, I didn't really have very much of a family life" (16). Is it, therefore, any wonder that the quest for recognition and acceptance could be correlated with the sense of abandonment the young Soupy felt? It is also instructive that what he characterizes as the "pivotal event of my life" – "playing the title role in my elementary school production of 'Peter Rabbit'" –

happens during this time. Reflecting on the "laughing and clapping" that ensued during his performance and how it would become a necessity in his life, he even hazards a psychoanalytic interpretation for why he may require the "constant reassurance, constant demonstrations of love" that being a comedian and performer would give him. "I knew that entertaining people (although only six at the time) was going to be my life" (17).

His life would begin to blossom as a consequence of the move from Franklinton to Huntington, West Virginia in 1934, a town with almost fifty times more people than the remote hamlet in North Carolina. In fact, the Jewish population of Huntington around the time of the move was about equal (1200) to Franklinton's total inhabitants. There were even two Jewish congregations although whether his family was a member of either one is unclear. What is clear, however, is that Soupy "took to Huntington like a duck to water" (18). If Soupy had felt like an ugly duckling in Franklinton because of the loss of his father and his Jewish background, Huntington provided a more hospitable environment, especially when it came to social interaction with other kids.

One of those childhood friends from Huntington, Bill Cravens, recalls that when Soupy moved into his neighborhood they immediately found a way to showcase Soupy's budding comedic talents. According to Cravens, "we used to put on shows for the neighborhood kids in his garage. I was the straight man and he was the comedian" (21). Cravens further remarks that Soupy would "send his joke material to comedians like Bob Hope and Red Skelton" (21). Although there was no indication that either responded to Soupy's comedic offers, it seems that Skelton, as the character of "Freddie the Freeloader," may have influenced Soupy's use of the battered top-hat that became part of his costume later on his lunchtime television program on WXYZ-TV in Detroit in the 1950s.

Soupy's own recollections from his school days in Huntington underscore how he was "an inveterate class cutup...with a little more personality than most" (22). While self-conscious about his appearance, Soupy, in the self-deprecating mode that would stamp his comedic persona and lead eventually to taking thousands of pies in the face, observes "if you looked like I did then you had to be funny" (22). Beyond the employment of facial expressions to convey humor, Soupy absorbed the physical comedy of the Marx Brothers and their "anarchic mayhem," (23) a mayhem that was integral to the slapstick *shticks* on Soupy's television shows in the 1950s and 1960s.

It was in high school where Soupy began to experiment with standup comedy, "stealing bits" (23) from other well-known comedians. Relying on radio and the movies to help develop his timing and delivery, he would use a variety of venues in and out of school to attract an audience and the acceptance and recognition that went with performing. Wordplay, in particular, was part of his standup comedy and would continue to be essential to his act and later television shows. One example of such wordplay that he recalls from those high school standup times is the following: "My mother and father are in the iron and steel business. My mother irons and my father steals" (24).

While comedy was the driving force behind his desire to perform, Soupy also dabbled in playing the clarinet and being an amateur journalist by "reviewing movies and bands" for the school newspaper (25). His love of swing music in this era of big band jazz would remain a constant in his life whether as a disc jockey on various radio stations from Cleveland to New York City or in what would become a very popular evening program on Detroit's WXYZ-TV, *Soupy's On*, that featured nationally prominent jazz musicians who were appearing at Motor City clubs or concert venues. Soupy was both a fan of the music and, as attested to later by others, an incredibly knowledgeable *aficionado* of big bands, jazz ensembles and soloists. According to one of his high school friends, Betty Ann Keen, she and Soupy "formed a fan club for the Jerry Wald Orchestra" (24) – a lesser known clarinetist who, like the much better known Artie Shaw and Benny Goodman, led a swing jazz band. Wald's aggregation, consisting of four trumpets, four trombones, and five saxophones, plus, of course, a rhythm section, had a large number of Jewish musicians, which may have also been an attraction for Soupy. His love of the music was further reinforced by his infatuation with swing dancing. Those dance steps would most likely make their reappearance in what emerged as the "Soupy Shuffle" on his WXYZ-TV noontime television show to be followed later in the national syndication of that show.

When he graduated Huntington High School in 1943, he immediately began classes at Marshall College located in Huntington. Continuing his journalism as a not very conscientious sports writer for the Marshall College student newspaper, his byline as "Suppy" Supman would appear only periodically. According to Soupy, the sports editor told him that he "was spending too much time delivering punch lines and not enough collecting bylines" (25). However, his career as a cub journalist and college student was cut short when he enlisted in the Navy at the age of seventeen after only one term at college.

The physical and psychological transition from a rather carefree environment to one wrought with the terrors of war had a profound impact on Soupy. Although he proffers the cliché that "the day I entered the Navy was the day I became a man" (29), his time in basic training and in service in the Pacific were punctuated by tragic moments that would remain, like an anchor (excuse the pun), to his generally buoyant personality. One of those moments which was too painful to describe was a "terrible airplane accident" (29) that happened during basic training in San Diego. Such moments represent what one neuroscientist calls "flashbulb memories," or ones that have such strong "emotional reactions" that they retain importance for one's life story (Schnider 2018: 176-7).

Soupy's reluctance to provide the specifics for that accident may also represent the trauma such an incident engendered. Without any more documentary references to the specifics or the actual time frame, I can only hazard a guess about the details. Given what exists in the military records and the particular time frame for Soupy's basic training, it appears that the horrific event took place on June 6, 1944 at the Naval Auxiliary Air Station in Kearny Mesa, just north of San Diego, where a navy plane crashed on takeoff killing eighteen and injuring another twelve. There was also a later crash that occurred shortly after takeoff from Lindbergh Field in San Diego on November 22, 1944 that killed all six of the crew onboard. Salzberg notes that Soupy's fear of flying is attributable to being part of a clean-up detail after that accident or the earlier one or one not in the military record but in Soupy's reconstructed memory of several different events (30).

Once Soupy began his service as a Seaman, First Class, on the U. S. S. *Randall*, an attack transport ship launched in 1944, he experienced many frightening moments. It is possible that the stories he recounts about serving during the invasion of Okinawa have the ring of narrative truth without accurately reflecting the historical truth of the role of the U. S. S. *Randall*. Apparently, that ship did transport men and material for the horrifying campaigns at Iwo Jima, Guam, and eventually Okinawa. However, that ship did not arrive in Okinawa until after the appalling atomic bomb attacks on Hiroshima and Nagasaki. Soupy also claims that the *Randall* "delivered the first atomic bomb to the Bikini atoll" (30). While the Bikini atoll was used for atomic and nuclear weapons, the testing did not start until after WWII in 1946. So, understandably, Soupy's recollections of the exploits of his ship during his time in the Navy blend into those embellished and even manufactured memories that often form part of any person's life stories.

On the other hand, Soupy's "warm memories" of being in the navy during WWII are rooted in "the wonderful camaraderie" and "bonds of friendship" experienced during his time onboard the ship (30). It was on the *Randall* where he also was able to entertain the other sailors "via the ship's onboard intercom" (30). Those performances, consisting mainly of telling jokes and playing music, would later become part of his regular repertoire on radio and television. Especially significant to his identity as a performer in children's television programming as "Soupy Sales" on WXYZ-TV in Detroit was his invention of the character of White Fang, an imaginary dog based on Jack London's character of the same name but having the growls and howls found on the V-Disc of the *Hound of the Baskervilles*. Admitting that he purloined the disc when he left the navy, Soupy claims that it was in Detroit where someone stole it from him (31).

Returning to Huntington after his naval service, Soupy continued his college education at Marshall and his radio and stand-up comedy performances. Those stand-up gigs were at dive bars in West Virginia and Ohio towns that were, in Soupy's words, "pretty seamy." He jokingly recalls that they "were the kinds of places where they played the 'Star Spangled Banner' every fifteen minutes just to see who could still stand up" (33). Elsewhere he observes that "joke telling (what we call stand-up comedy today) fell somewhere between taking tickets and cleaning up after the circus elephants on the show business hierarchy...Stand-up comics told their jokes in bars and speakeasies. I know because I experienced it first hand" (Sales 2003: 123).

One of those seedy places at which he performed stand-up comedy that he identified as his "first professional gig...was in a bar in Mansfield, Ohio, called the Ringside." Although Soupy claims it was named that because "heavyweight-boxing champ Rocky Marciano once came in for an evening" (Sales 2003: 124), it is difficult to either verify the story or, indeed, even the time line. What has some historical validity is that Rocky Marciano was heavyweight champion in the late 1940s through the early 1950s. (In fact, Marciano defeated Detroit's own magnificent heavyweight champion, Joe Louis, on October 27, 1951 in Louis's last match of an otherwise stellar and significant boxing career.)

Although these performances took place under rather challenging circumstances, Soupy honed his skill at one-liners and contending with the heckling that sometimes interrupted his act. Once while emceeing for a stripper at the Ringside who insisted that he gather up the silver dollars thrown onstage for her, he wound up getting into a physical altercation with an irate patron who did not appreciate either Soupy's act or his comeback to the heckling. Actually, the fight, according to Soupy, was more of a first-round knockout since the guy floored Soupy with one punch, a punch that had the audience in stitches while he recovered from his injuries in the dressing room. As he sardonically notes, "I wasn't particularly crazy about working in front of a live club audience" (35).

Radio, in fact, became his métier and "training ground" for what would become a lifelong career as a comedic entertainer and television personality. After graduating from Marshall with a degree in journalism in 1949, Soupy secured a position at WHTN, one of the main radio stations in Huntington. Initially writing copy for commercials, he eventually was able to do his own radio show, "called 'Wax Works,' which was a couple of hours a day...(where he would) be spinning records, telling jokes, selling time, and writing commercials" (38-9). Making the princely sum of around $250 a week, Soupy transitioned not only into the professional world of media performer but also into married life. He blithely recounts his courtship and marriage to Barbara Fox, "an aspiring singer and model," endowed with a necessary "good sense of humor." Soupy's humor is evident when he explains that the marriage was about getting "hitched but not to a post" (39).

After his show on WHTN was cancelled in 1950, "Suppy" Supman, as he was referred to at the time, got a call from the former general manager of the Huntington radio station who now was working in television in Cincinnati. The television station, WKRC, owned by the famous Taft family, hired "Suppy." At the "station's request" he changed his name to "Soupy Hines," the last name for a local soup company and not the for the better-known Heinz variation (43). What Soupy proposed to WKRC-TV that made it to the air in late 1950 and early 1951 represented one of the first television dance programs. *Soupy's Soda Shop* ran alternatively for an hour and then half hour from 5:30-6:30 and 6:00 to 6:30 P.M. each day during the week. Writing and producing the show, Soupy played mostly his much loved Big Band numbers, interviewing the kids in between the musical selections. Soupy also did another show, called *Club Nothing*, which featured the kind of sketch comedy that would later be part of his shows in Detroit, Los Angeles, and New York City. The Cincinnati

Enquirer listed that show as running either for an hour from 10-11 P.M. or for forty-five minutes from 11:45-12:30 P.M. through March of 1951. Soupy remarks that those "comedy sketches and interviews" he did were "sort of a forerunner of the *Tonight Show*" (44).

Both shows were cancelled in the spring of 1951. Reflecting on those cancellations with some bitterness about the "used car dealer" mentality exhibited by the station managers, Soupy deploys the names of certain television personalities to critique the narrow and misguided mindset that fostered such decisions. While inaccurately identifying the connections and contexts for his critique, Soupy, nonetheless, makes some intriguing insights into the capriciousness of television programming. According to Soupy, the "flunkies" who cancelled his dance show did so because "Nobody wants to see a bunch of teenagers dance" (44). As a biting retort to this decision, Soupy cites the success of Dick Clark and *American Bandstand* happening only six months later (44-45). Although Clark and that show did attain both prominence and longevity, *American Bandstand* did not appear on the air until 1956, lasting until 1989. Another person who worked at WKRC-TV as a writer of dramas was Rod Serling, later of *Twilight Zone* fame. Soupy claims that he was fired on the same day as Rod Serling. However, according to the *Cincinnati Enquirer*, Serling's local shows went on for months after Soupy's shows were terminated.

Fortunately for Soupy, he rebounded quickly by securing a job as a deejay at WJW, a Cleveland radio station in May of 1951. First working from 6 to 9 A.M. at what would become to be called a morning drive show, Soupy also did some afternoon programming that relied on his comedic flair for telling jokes and doing crazy skits. Soupy refers to one of his most famous colleagues at WJW who was hired in July of 1951 and whose early evening radio show came on after Soupy's 4:30 to 5:00 P.M. time slot. Taking the moniker of "Moondog" as his WJW persona, Alan Freed would be the first "mainstream" disc jockey, meaning white dj, to play rhythm and blues (R & B) on radio. Freed would go on to coin the term "rock 'n' roll" although there had been references to "rocking and rolling" in so-called "race" music and records back in the 1920s up through R & B songs in the 1940s. Freed advanced the concept and the music through his radio show and the concerts he promoted. For Soupy, it was a revelation that such an increasingly popular media personality could get away with, as Soupy saw it, doing "his show drunk just about every night" (46).

Soupy Hines publicity photo from pre-Detroit radio and television roles

If not as successful as "Moondog" with his radio program and local appearances, Soupy, nonetheless, would make the rounds at local events for promotional purposes. The *Cleveland Plain Dealer* listed Soupy's public appearances in conjunction with numerous other local disc jockeys at a high school jamboree event in January of 1952 and with pop singer, Alan Dale, at the Halle Brothers record department in July of 1952 as, of course, Soupy Hines.

It was as Soupy Hines that he started on WXEL-TV in Cleveland in 1952 with a weekly half hour show from 11 to 11:30 A.M. called *Soup's On.* (This would later morph into a slight variation as *Soupy's On,* his evening WXYZ-TV program that expanded from an initial fifteen-minute time slot at 11 P.M. in late 1953 into a regular thirty minute show through 1959). The program often featured Soupy pantomiming to records and showcasing popular singers. It was also on that television show that Soupy began a *shtick* that would become an iconic signature of Soupy Sales comedy - the pie in the face.

This particular routine, a parody of the 1950 movie *Broken Arrow,* required filming outdoors and having Soupy play a certain Native American chief. In the film in which whites continued to perform as "Indians," the actor Jeff Chandler portrayed Cochise, the famous Chiricahua Apache who resisted U. S. encroachment on his lands from 1861-1872. (It should be pointed out, however, that this movie actually did employ a Canadian Mohawk actor, Jay Silverheels, to play Geronimo, perhaps as an attempt to show greater racial tolerance, especially in the aftermath of WWII. Silverheels would go on to become the television version of "Tonto" in *The Lone Ranger,* based on the nationally-syndicated Detroit-based WXYZ radio program of the same name.) In the bit, Soupy as the "Indian" chief is supposed to be on a horse except that he gets thrown off. Picking himself up, he, nonetheless, speaks the following lines: "Soldier come to Indian country. You kill our buffalo, you kill our antelope, you shoot our deer, what is left for the Indian?" The answer comes in the form of a pie in the face with Soupy uttering through the fluff on his face: "That's not what I had in mind" (48). (If only Native peoples had to contend with getting pies in their face instead of the genocide inflicted on them for centuries, there might have been a much less violent and tragic confrontation between them and the merciless expanding U. S. white supremacist empire.)

It appears that *Soup's On* soon suffered a minor version of the displacement that the Indigenous of North America confronted. The show was cancelled. The ongoing arguments with the program director at WJW also led to Soupy leaving Cleveland radio land. However, with a wife and small child (Tony, born on September 26, 1951), Soupy still shuffled around Cleveland trying to make a living as an entertainer. In the January 9, 1953 edition of the *Cleveland Plain Dealer* there is a reference to Soupy Hines doing a beer commercial in between the Wednesday night TV broadcasts of boxing. Also, there is a March 1, 1953 announcement of an appearance by Soupy at a local club, "Moe's Main Street," with the singer Betty Ann Clooney. At least one review of Soupy's stand-up in the *Cleveland Plain Dealer* on March 6, 1953 was unremitting in its vitriol (with perhaps a smattering of anti-Semitism to boot): "He nearly wrecks the Main Street's small stage with his violent nonsense. His monkey-like take offs are as boisterous as his horrible puns; yet the Hines fans seem to love it when he dives into the corn silo" (28). For this critic, his corniness would not be missed as Soupy exited the Cleveland stage for Detroit in the spring of 1953.

Not only would his time in Detroit lead to an incredible growth in his popularity and following, including a national breakout for his children's television show, but also it would, ironically, bring about his replacement of Betty Clooney in the WXYZ-TV time slot of 11 P.M. with *Soupy's On*. Before considering the specifics of those television shows on WXYZ-TV, I want to look at the role of television and popular culture in the 1950s as another way of situating Soupy Sales and his shows in the social and cultural context of the times.

CHAPTER TWO

TELEVISION AND POPULAR CULTURE
IN THE 1950S

When the twenty-seven year old Soupy Hines arrived in Detroit in the spring of 1953, his prior experiences in commercial television in Cincinnati and Cleveland only partially prepared him for his multiple programming roles at WXYZ-TV, the local ABC affiliate. The general manager of that Detroit television station, John Pival, recalled seeing Soupy do stand-up comedy in Cincinnati and invited him to audition. The audition became, in effect, a rehearsal for a kids' show that would air at noontime five days a week (Castelnero 2009: 12-13). According to Soupy, "John Pival wanted a show where I'd have lunch with the kids every day. I didn't have any experience working with kids (remember, those 'kids' in Cincinnati were teenagers) but then again, there weren't actually going to be any kids on the show, just watching it" (Sales 2001: 53). And watch it they did! In the process, Soupy and his *Lunch with Soupy Sales* (known during the first few years as *12 O'clock Comics)* would become immensely popular with youngsters in the Motor City and eventually around the country when it gained national syndication in 1959 on Saturday afternoon.

While Chapters Four and Five will discuss Soupy's shows within the context of the Detroit experience during the seven years (1953-1960) of his various starring roles on WXYZ-TV, this chapter will focus on the national picture of television and popular culture in the 1950s. In particular, identifying the institutional and ideological constraints on television and popular culture during this period should provide both the historical and social grounding for what cultural historian, Elaine Tyler May, calls "Cold War Containment." The domestic expression of this containment "was bolstered by a powerful political culture that marked its adherents and marginalized its detractors" (May 2008: 16). Advertising, as we will see in this chapter, deployed the apprehensions and dread induced by the Cold War to sell consumer products and Cold War ideology. A number of major corporations in the late 1940s and early 1950s gave millions of their own advertising revenues to boost ads that also promoted "the American Economic system to the American people, under the assumption that if they better understood how the economy functioned, they would also work harder for its success and be less vulnerable to 'disturbers and communists'" (Grieve 2018: 128-29 and 17).

The interaction between television as a medium of commercial and consumer values and the domestic routines legitimized through institutions like the family and education will be one of the other topics to be explored in this chapter (Boddy 1990: 20; Hilmes 2014: 166-239). How television became so integral to the operation of the domestic household is an essential element in understanding not only the attraction of Soupy Sales's lunchtime show but also the ways in which popular culture was shaped by economic and social factors. "Television," as Susan Murray notes, "reimagined many traditional forms of popular culture, adapting them to suit its particular needs and strengths" (Murray 2005: 42). Among those specific roles that television performed was as "a domestic medium (whereby) the routines of viewing are part of the domestic routines by which home life is organized" (Fiske 2011: 72).

That organization of domestic life was reinforced by the placement of television sets in a prime location in the home (Spigel 1992: 37-39). Invariably this meant that the TV would be prominently displayed in the living room. According to a 1954 national survey, eighty-five percent of respondents identified the living room as the prime location for their TV sets (Spigel 1992: 68). Without exception among the nearly two-dozen interviews I conducted with those who watched Soupy's WXYZ-TV shows, their U. S. manufactured television set (Motorola, Zenith, etc.) was strategically situated in the living room.

For a few of those who ate lunch with Soupy in the kitchen, their TV sets would have to swivel in order to be viewed from that vantage point. Thus, television's intrusion into domestic living arrangements resulted in new kinds of furniture, including TV tray tables that first made their appearance in national advertising in 1952 and 1953 (Marling 1994: 188). A number of the interviewees attested to the use of TV tray tables when they were given permission to eat in the living room.

Mother and kids in the Living Room with 1950's Television Set

As a commercial industry, television was intimately connected to postwar business operations that reflected the various interests of electronic manufacturers, broadcast networks and their sponsors. As the electronics industry shifted from war to domestic production, it relied on the sales of television sets to assure its profits. By 1950, television sets dominated more than half of the total sales in the U. S. electronic industry with RCA, because of monopolistic licensing agreements, being guaranteed 3.5 percent of every sale (Boddy 1990: 31 and 3). Television sets were selling at the rate of five million a year during the 1950s, leading to 87 percent of families owning a television by 1960 (Coontz 2000: 25).

Beyond the purchase of television sets, networks acted as marketing mechanisms for an expanding consumer economy. TV networks "provided a relentless flow of information and persuasion that placed acts of consumption at the core of everyday life" (Lipsitz 1990: 47 and 44-5). The federal government facilitated the commercial and consumer roles of television by enacting specific policies through the

Federal Communications Commission (FCC) that benefitted the networks and their advertising practices. The FCC decisions, especially during the years from 1948-1952, ensured that advertising would have a privileged position in the day-to-day operations of network television. This led editorial writers like Walter Lippmann to castigate television for becoming the "servant of merchandising." (Boddy 1990: 259). Underscoring this merchandising mission of television, another opinion piece in the December 1959 edition of a TV industry journal maintained, "Television, because of its tremendous hold on the American public, its power as a communications medium, has merely highlighted the symbolic ills of advertising" (Boddy 1990: 250).

Beyond the endless corporate sponsorship of television advertising, those very same commercial interests attempted to exercise an insidious guiding hand to the scripts on a wide variety of 1950s television shows. Advertisers like Proctor & Gamble, the leading sponsor of television programming, would urge writers to avoid any scenes that would "contribute negatively to the public morale" (Boddy, 1990: 199). In fact, there were times when advertisers would exercise forms of censorship on scripts that even hinted at a reference to a competing company or product. According to Rod Serling, who provided many scripts to the TV dramas in the 1950s, one absurd example of such censorship was a line in a show sponsored by Chevrolet that excised a reference to "ford" a river (Boddy 1990: 201).

Like other television personalities of the 1950s, Soupy promoted a wide array of products on his shows on WXYZ-TV from Jell-O and Faygo, a local soda pop favorite, during the day to the Detroit-produced Altes beer during the evening. According to one study of television personalities, "by the mid 50s, the selling and merchandising of one's own persona had become an absolutely essential component of a television star's career" (Murray 2005: ix). Although the adoption of Soupy's last name, "Sales," after the movie comic, Chic Sale, came at the suggestion of John Pival, the often ham-fisted hucksterism required by TV performers, like Soupy, added another unintended layer of meaning to his new last name. The inveterate young viewers of Soupy's lunchtime program, in particular, would insist that their moms purchase the very food items Soupy would advertise for his lunch on the following day. These food items, like Jell-O, were often attached to specific sponsors of the show. Peggy Tibbits was one of those kids who would urge her mom to buy and prepare the lunch according to Soupy's menu, becoming unknowingly an enabler of the commercial interests of the program (Castelnero 2009: 11-12).

Other network children's shows, like *Howdy Doody*, and popular TV characters, like Hopalong Cassidy, promoted a variety of products. On the *Howdy Doody* show, Buffalo Bob, the avuncular announcer, urged the kids watching the program to "have your Mom or Daddy take you to the store where you get Poll Parrot shoes, and ask for your Howdy Doody cutout." Hopalong Cassidy, the first of numerous stars of western TV series spawned in the 1950s, marketed a long list of products from "pajamas, wallpaper, candy bars, watches, toothpaste tubes, and cowboy paraphernalia produced by over one hundred companies to the tune of $70 million annually" (Engelhardt 1986: 71).

Network executives were eager to cash in on this marketing bonanza. In particular, they adjusted their program operations based on their sense of the 1950s preferred demographic. Leonard Goldenson, President of ABC, said about the connections between programming and demographics in the mid 1950s, "We're after a specific audience, the young housewife...with two to four kids, who has to buy the clothing, the food, the soaps, and the home remedies" (Quoted in Boddy 1990: 155). It is not surprising that the dominant ideology of this period favored large families and stay-at-home mothers. As argued by feminist TV social critic, Lynn Spigel, "The 1950s was a decade that invested an enormous amount of cultural capital in the ability to form a family and live out a set of highly structured gender and generational roles...In this social climate, television was typically welcomed as a catalyst for renewed domestic values" (Spigel 1992: 2). In line with this emphasis on stay-at-home moms, the early ads for Soupy's *12 O'clock Comics* show were on the so-called "Woman's Page" of the *Detroit Free Press.*

Nonetheless, as much as television and other media promoted the idea of the stay-at-home mom, many women entered the workforce at certain times during the 1950s out of economic necessity. Surprisingly, there were two million more wives at work in 1952 than during WWII peak production. Yet, the cultural push to domesticate women by driving them into both motherhood and household servant was particularly evident in a 1954 article in *Esquire* that called working wives a "menace" (Coontz 2000: 31-32). While 1950 television sit-coms also reflected this domestic containment ideology, there were, at times, both contradictory media messages and compelling needs for women to seek employment. One of my interviewees who had his lunch with Soupy recalled that his mom began part-time work as a United Automobile Workers (UAW) secretary around the same time in 1959 when his father, a member of the United Steelworkers of

America (USWA), went on the almost five month strike conducted by the USWA in that same year. His dad also prepared many of the meals during lunchtime in 1959, in effect, substituting for the role his mom previously occupied.

Children became ever more attached to the growing number of television shows geared to young people, especially during early morning, noon, after school weekdays and on Saturday morning. During the 1950s children's television programming went from 2.5 hours per week to a high of 37 hours per week in 1956 (Pecora *et. al.* 2007: 8-9). There was a mixed reaction to the impact television and its programming would have on the kids "although studies published in the early 1950s exuded a sense of optimism...,claiming that TV was reuniting families, increasing social interaction among family members, and increasing children's store of information about the world" (Luke 1990: 108). Reflecting this sense of optimism, the *New York Times* in 1951 opined, "Youngsters today need television for their morale as much as they need fresh air and sunshine for their health" (Lipsitz 1990: 53). Some audience research indicated that parents thought television performed a valuable service in "keeping their children off the streets" even as other adults believed that kids were becoming "victims of the new pied piper" (Spigel 1992: 50 and 45).

The fact is that children, like other viewers of TV shows, are not just passive receptacles, mindlessly incorporating the messages of this seemingly invasive medium. Depending on their ages, class, ethnicity, gender and other social and psychological factors, kids translate what they see on television into their own play (Tullock 2000: 149). Although "television-as-culture" attempts to produce "preferred meanings that perform the work of the dominant ideology" for any and every audience, including children, that diversified audience finds ways of constructing its own meanings within particular social and cultural constraints, creating in the process a "multiplicity of meanings" (Fiske 2011: 15 and 1-2) and the potential for an "oppositional culture" because of unfulfilled desires formed by TV and popular culture (Lipsitz 1990: 17).

Nevertheless, the strong arm of the dominant ideology imposed a conformist message that permeated television programming during much of the 1950s. The close connections between corporate interests, network advertisers, and the anti-communist ideology of the period led to political repression and blacklisting, especially following the publication in 1950 of *Red Channels: The Report on Communist Influence in Radio and Television* (Boddy 1990: 99-100; Murray 2005:

107; and Nadel 2005: 36-37). Certainly, blacklisting of political dissidents and suspect others was not limited to television performers but encompassed a wide range of occupations from teachers to union activists (Schrecker 1998). However, the numerous examples of egregious political blacklisting in television led to tragic conclusions for many of those performers subjected to such repression. When *Red Channels* accused Phillip Loeb, the actor who played Jack Goldberg in the tremendously popular early 1950s TV program, *The Goldbergs*, of suspicious subversive tendencies, such as petitioning for the integration of professional baseball, pressure was put on the producers to drop Loeb from the show. Gertrude Berg, one of the producers and leading actor in the show, capitulated to threats by sponsors to pull all their advertising unless Loeb was fired. Not only did he lose his job on *The Goldbergs*, but also the blacklisting in the television industry that followed him for several years led to his tragic suicide in 1956 (Lipsitz 1990: 62-63; and Nesteroff 2015: 119-20).

Other performers were fired and blacklisted because their prior political activities disrupted the attempt by sponsors to prevent controversy from tainting the programs with which they were associated. Mady Christians's engagement with refugees fleeing fascism in the 1930s and 1940s was used against her effort to re-enact the same role in the TV production of *I Remember Mama* that she did in the Broadway play (Lipsitz 1990: 63). Jerry Fielding, the musical director of Groucho Marx's show, *You Bet Your Life*, was fired from the show at the insistence of one of its sponsors, Chrysler. Fielding's political activism in support of equal pay for Blacks and whites in unions may have scared Chrysler because of its own employment of a large number of Black autoworkers whose pay was not equal to whites in the company (Nesteroff 2015: 115-16). A few very high-profile television performers were spared being blacklisted because of their popularity, especially with the very political forces enabling the repression. When Lucille Ball was called to testify before the House Un-American Activities Committee (HUAC) in 1953, HUAC committee members overlooked certain "communist" indiscretions in the past because they, and even J. Edgar Hoover, head of the FBI, were big fans of *I Love Lucy*.

While even establishment fans of television personalities like Lucille Ball could overlook their suspect backgrounds, such amateur viewers of TV shows were often totally unaware of or uninterested in the inner workings of the medium as a representation of the entertainment industry. Yet, for those in the industry and particularly ambitious young performers like Soupy Sales, taking account of which comedians achieved success as television personalities was of utmost interest.

It is indisputable that stand-up comedy and its practitioners, especially Jewish comedians, had a major impact on shaping television programming and the comedy variety shows in the 1950s (Marc 1997: 15-16). Their effect on other comic performers, like Soupy Sales, will be even more evident in the discussion in later chapters. For now, I want to explore how the comedy of Milton Berle and Sid Caesar, in particular, re-interpreted the stand-up comedy routines and Vaudeville *shticks* they brought with them into their television shows and why it attracted and repelled different audiences.

Milton Berle, born Mendel Berlinger in 1908, was part of a large cohort of comedians who were born and raised in New York City. Those comic performers, George Burns, Sid Caesar, and Phil Silvers, among others, would have a major impact on the television comedy shows of the 1950s. Berle, like the others, sharpened his comedic skills in burlesque, acting in variety shows in theatres and radio during the 1930s and 1940s. It was his background in vaudevillian type variety shows that he incorporated into what would become the roaring success of the Texaco Star Theatre in 1948, a success that made his Tuesday night time slot the most watched program on television but would also lead to numerous criticisms of his "vulgarity" (Murray 2005: 55-58; and Spigel 1992: 145-50). According to one study of the impact of Berle's TV show in Detroit, "water levels dropped in the city's reservoir immediately after the show when the viewers rushed to their bathrooms" (Epstein 2001: 130). As one columnist noted, "Berle's rapid gags, broad clowning, versatility, and hard work added up to video's first smash hit" (Quoted in Epstein 2001: 131).

Milton Berle & Texaco Star Theatre Promotional Ad

Acting as the master of ceremonies and comedic prankster throughout the show, Berle was not unlike those Jewish jesters known in Yiddish as *tummlers* who oversaw the entertainment on the Borscht Belt circuit in those resorts in the Catskills frequented especially by New York City Jews (Berger 2001: 58; DesRechers 2014: 22-23; and Nachman 2003: 23-29). In her incisive study of Jewish humor throughout the ages and in different cultures, Ruth Wisse identified the Borscht Belt as "an incubator of a new form of entertainment that gradually emerged from its formative center into the U. S. mainstream and beyond" (Wisse 2013: 126). While Soupy had not played the Borscht Belt, he certainly was, as other Jewish comics, influenced by it as it radiated outwards. In addition, he avoided Yiddish, perhaps as a consequence of its lack in his background and the particular audiences for which he performed. Berle, nonetheless, reveled in Yiddish and used it throughout his early shows as the *tummler* in charge of NBC's *Texaco Star Theatre*. Exclaiming in one bit, "I'm *schvitzing* in here," referring to how he was sweating in the outfit he wore, Berle relied on other Yiddish words and Jewish humor.

After moving to New York in the early 1960s and performing there for most of the rest of his life, Soupy may have discovered the value of using Yiddish as a punch line in a funny Jewish-inflected story like the following he included in his collection of jokes, entitled *Stop Me If You've Heard It!:*

> *A guy gets a new dog, a nice Jewish dog, so he calls him Einstein. He can't wait to show off the dog to his neighbor. So, a couple of weeks later when the neighbor finally comes over the guy calls Einstein into the house, bragging about how smart he is. The dog quickly comes running and stands looking up at his master; tail wagging excitedly, mouth open, tongue hanging out, eyes bright with anticipation. The guy points to the newspaper on the couch and commands, "Fetch!"*
>
> *Immediately, the dog climbs up on the couch, his doggie smile disappears, and he stops wagging his tail and starts to frown. Looking at his master he whines, "you think this is easy, wagging my tail all the time? Oy, vey. This constant wagging of the tail puts me in such pain, you should only know!*
>
> *And you think it's easy eating that dreck you call designer dog food? Forget it...it's too salty and it gives me gas, but what do you care? Then you push me out the door twice a day to take care of my business-disgusting, I tell you!"*
>
> *The neighbor is absolutely stunned. In astonishment he says, "I can't believe it. Einstein can speak! You asked him to fetch the newspaper and he is sitting on the sofa talking to us!" "Yes, I know, but" says the dog owner, "he's not fully trained yet. He thought I said, 'kvetch'"* (Sales 2003: 171).

Relying on vaudeville routines that made him a target of slapstick pranks, Berle would have an obvious influence on Soupy's television persona, especially the ways that "(Berle's) awkward physicality and psychological vulnerability (were) expressed through his self-deprecating humor" (Murray 2005: 68). In addition, there were links between the gags performed on Berle's syndicated evening program and those executed on Soupy's noontime show. For example, although Berle did take a pie in the face now and then, it was more often the case that someone would pummel him with giant powder puff whenever anyone called out "makeup" (Epstein 2001: 132). Berle's mugging through being drenched with seltzer may have provided the inspiration for a bit on Soupy's set where whenever he would pull a plug from a wall with a sign reading "Do Not Touch," he would be doused with a stream of water.

There were other common threads that connected Berle to Soupy. Both at times would play directly to the camera although Berle, more often than not, was in costume for his mugging close-ups. Also like Soupy, Berle performed live, but in front of a large audience. Soupy's audience consisted of the stagehands on the WXYZ-TV set. They often burst into laughter at the various *shticks* and gags that made up the routines on the noontime show. Where Berle's television persona would overlap especially with Soupy's was in his reference to being an "Uncle Miltie" to the kids watching his show. In that role he administered advice to kids, urging them to be "good little boys and girls" (Epstein 2001: 133). Being older than Soupy, the "Uncle" appellation would become attached to Berle. Soupy, on the other hand, seemed less like a crazy uncle than a silly older brother who also, nevertheless, gave advice in the form of Soupy's "Words of Wisdom."

Pinky Lee, born Pincus Leff in 1907, was another Jewish comic contemporary of Milton Berle and Soupy Sales who utilized the style and pace of vaudeville, first in a television variety show and then in a dedicated children's show, syndicated on NBC stations on Saturday morning in 1954 and 1955. "I played the same little guy on TV that I did in the burlesque...I was what you call a nebbish, a pathetic little guy" (Grossman 1987: 118). Nebbish or not, Pinky Lee was as loud as Berle and as physical as Soupy. He also performed a little dance number, similar to Soupy, as part of his opening sequence. More like Berle, however, critics attacked Lee for his "tasteless exploits" and engendering of "hysterical bedlam" (Grossman 1987: 118-19).

As the viewers for Berle, in particular, grew, they moved beyond those urban areas that made up a sizeable segment of his audience in the period from 1949-1952. Some estimates suggest that as much as thirty-five percent of that audience resided in New York City (Epstein 2001: 134). According to some of the more conservative critics, "vaudeville humor did not appeal to Midwestern audiences" and by 1953 Texaco withdrew its sponsorship of Berle's show, resulting ultimately in its cancellation in 1955 (Spigel 1992: 147-150). Even more malicious with perhaps a tinge of anti-Semitism, the radio commentator Paul Harvey criticized television broadcasts that emanated from New York City for "contaminating an awful lot of fresh air." For Harvey, the culprits were "New York comedians" who spread a "virus" that had to be expunged (Spigel 1992: 114).

One of those other viral New York comedians who infected the television airways and popular culture around the country was Sid Caesar. Born in 1922 in Yonkers, New York to Max and Ida Ziser,

Jewish immigrants from Eastern Europe, Caesar marched through the Catskills, like his namesake did in crossing the Rubicon, to become, in effect, an Emperor of the Television Airwaves. Having trained in the Catskills, Caesar used his talent with voices and characters to attract a dedicated audience. *Your Show of Shows* ran from 1950-1954 on NBC, achieving accolades and awards. It relied on the kind of sketch comedy that showcased Caesar, his supporting cast of Carl Reiner, Imogene Coca, and Howie Morris and what would become an amazing stable of comedy writers that included Mel Brooks, Larry Gelbart, Lucille Kallen, and Neil Simon (Berger 2001: 73-77; Epstein 2001: 138-44; and Nachman 2003: 100-22). As one critic noted, "he was wholly dependent on writers who, in turn, took inspiration from him" (Quoted in Nachman 2003: 100).

Caesar's sketch comedy, the movie parodies, and characters, like the various professors who proffered their hilarious absurdities, drew on both the anxieties of the present and angst of the past, creating in the process what Nanette Fabray, one of his co-stars, identified as "the first original TV comedy creation" (Nachman 2003: 101). From Lawrence Epstein's perspective "Caesar was a symbol of his time... Caesar's characters located the dark undersides of the vibrant, new America. Presented through humor, they were acceptable to audiences who were themselves grappling to control those undersides and build a postwar society" (Epstein 2001: 141-42). Yet Caesar's comedy and characters retained a residual Jewish humor that would be expressed especially by the goofy-looking professors whose disheveled frock coat and battered top hat gave the appearance of a displaced hobo, or, more in keeping with the Jewish sensibility – a *luftmensch*. (If you don't have a clue about what this term means, just check out one of the many floating male figures in any of the paintings of the Russian Jewish artist, Marc Chagall.)

One of these professors was Ludwig Von Sedative, a German sounding "expert" whose Yiddish inflections and inane counsel recalled the *rebbes* in the "Wise Men of Chelm," the Jewish folk tales of *shtetl* simpletons. Here is Professor Von Sedative's take on sleep: "Schleep is vunderbar. Schleep is beautiful. But schleep is no good to you if you is vide avake." While the professor first hails his friend who "could schleep anyveres....He could go on a train and right avay he fall aschleep." When the interviewer remarks how "wonderful that is," the Professor's comedic comeback is that it "was lousy. He was the engineer. He wrecked more trains, dot friend of mine" (Berger 2001: 80-1)

Another professor, Ludwig von Fossil, a so-called expert in archaeology, seemed to come closest to the spirit of foolish Chelm *rebbes* when he explained the results of his attempt to straighten out the Leaning Tower of Pisa. Assembling a large caravan of camels and tying a rope to their humps, they pulled and pulled for days. When queried about the outcome, he blithely responded that there was no change in the Leaning Tower of Pisa, but all the humps in the camels had been flattened (Nachman 2003: 104-105).

It was characters like these professors and others performed by Caesar and his cast, especially in their parodies, who would inspire Soupy Sales to try out such satirical sketches with similarly silly names on his evening show, *Soupy's On*. (Chapter Five will detail such characters and the supporting cast members.) Combining the comedic craziness of both Caesar and Berle, while stealing bits from others (as will be seen in Chapter Four), rooted him in specific styles of humor that zigged and zagged between what the comedian Richard Lewis referred to as Berle's "wacky funny" and Caesar's "torturously funny" (Nachman 2003: 101).

While the inspiration and influence of Jewish comedians and humor would inform, in part, the various routines that Soupy enacted on his daytime and evening television shows, it was the another kids program on 1950s television to which I now want to turn. Given how many of the baby-boomers who ate their lunch with Soupy also watched the *Mickey Mouse Club* (in my interviews of this age cohort it was almost unanimous), I believe reviewing this highly popular show will offer, by contrast to the Jewish vaudevillian sensibility of Soupy and Pinky Lee, further insight into the cold war containment and conformity that marked the dominant institutions and ideology of the period.

A primary motivation for the *Mickey Mouse Club* was Walt Disney's need to help underwrite the developing plans for his massive Southern California amusement park. Disneyland would open three months before the airing of the television show on October 3, 1955. In one of the first proposals for the program from September 1953, it was very evident that the *Mickey Mouse Club* and Disneyland would be intimately linked. For Disney, the theme park would be "everything a child has ever imagined, even in his wildest dreams" (Cotter 1997: 181). The television show would boost the park by locating it on an island set aside for the Mickey Mouse Club International Headquarters, reflecting the aspiring global reach of U. S. cultural products and fantasies. Also, through television, viewers could become citizens of

Disneyland with its normative validation of the American family (Nadel 2005: 49). As Steven Watts contends in his discussion of the *Mickey Mouse Club* in his book, *The Magic Kingdom*, aptly subtitled *Walt Disney and the American Way of Life*, the ABC afternoon program became "one of the great fads of 1950s American popular culture" (Watts 1997: 337).

However, it took a little convincing and a lot of lobbying before ABC finally offered 2.5 million dollars for the production of a one hour series to air five days a week. Although ABC and Walt Disney Productions had previously in April 1954 negotiated a seven-year contract for special television programming, a daily TV children's show was another matter. Bill Walsh, the producer of two prior Disney television Christmas specials in 1950 and 1951, was tasked with creating a children's program for the late afternoon time slot on ABC that would continue the connections between television programming and the theme park (Nadel 2005: 44-45; and Watts 1997: 377-82). The original prospectus envisioned a live studio audience. However, that idea was abandoned in favor of an ensemble of child performers. These kid-next-door types were to be designated as "Mouseketeers," adorned with black felt Mickey Mouse hats with protruding ears. Each of the Mouseketeers would shout out their first names that adorned the shirts they wore just in case their most youthful viewers couldn't read. Those viewers, both children and adults, would be greeted by Disney animated figures singing the lyrics, highlighted by being spelled-out, that would resonate for years to come: "Who's the leader of the club that's made for you and me?/ M-I-C-K-E-Y M-O-U-S-E./Hey there, hi there, ho there, you're as welcome as can be./M-I-C-K-E-Y M-O-U-S-E" (Watts 1997: 336).

The assembly of child performers was divided into three teams, Red, White, and Blue, reflecting a patriotic salute to the American flag. In turn, they would share their duties as happy-go-lucky Mouseketeers. Ironically, it was the Red Team that won the allegiance of the majority of the television audience, estimated by 1956 to be over 14 million viewers (Cotter 1997: 183-86). It was also determined that as many as one-third of those viewers were adults. Perhaps those adults were "busy mothers" who would "welcome a daily babysitter," giving them "a much needed break by entertaining and instructing their children." Embedded in that entertainment was a strict moral code upheld by "good Mouseketeers (who) always respected the authority of teachers, policemen, and parents" (Watts 1997: 343).

The lead adult in the *Mickey Mouse Club,* Jimmie Dodd, provided religiously tinged instruction to the viewers of the show. As president of the Hollywood Christian Group, Dodd offered a kind of Norman Vincent Peale rendition of religion mixing "traditional values with positive thinking." This was especially transparent in what came to be known as "Doddisms" that contained "particular emphasis on the power of prayer" (Watts 1997: 343-44). According to one of the kids on the Red Team who accepted Dodd as the genial and gentile father figure, "He was a good Christian man…He liked working with kids. He and his wife could not have children, so we were his children" (Watts 1997: 337). Dodd was avidly pursued as a national speaker. In those speeches, he delivered assurances to parents that the cast all had backgrounds of "normal, stable, wholesome family life" and they would definitely act as a corrective to the "suggestive" lyrics of rock-and-roll" (Watts 1997: 344).

Indeed, the *Mickey Mouse Club* stood out against the raucous humor and slapstick routines performed by Pinky Lee and Soupy Sales during this same time in the mid to late 1950s. Although Soupy would have a hit song and dance called, "Do the Mouse," in the mid-1960s, it had more in common with his wild Soupy shuffle from the *Lunch with Soupy Sales* show than with the sedate and constrained dancing of the Mouseketeers. While Soupy studiously avoided references to politics and religion, he did dispense his own secular and jocular "Words of Wisdom." One example, written in chalk on a blackboard on Soupy's lunchtime set, was "Be true to your teeth and they won't be false to you." In stark contrast, one could not miss the obvious religious and Cold War political messaging in the *Mickey Mouse Club* whether it was the sign above the Clubhouse door that read "God Bless the Mickey Mouse Club" or the special segment on "Inside the FBI" which highlighted the agency's pursuit of subversive spies (Watts 1997: 343).

Perhaps, in a fitting gesture to the ironies inherent in the Cold War political messaging of the *Mickey Mouse Club,* Stanley Kubrick choose to end his 1987 film, *Full Metal Jacket*, with U. S. troops lustily singing the theme song to the show while they are framed by a bombed-out Vietnamese city, ablaze in the background. Given that many scholars see the Vietnam War as an inevitable and tragic extension of the Cold War (Appy 2015), it's not surprising to hear the "Mickey Mouse March" being sung, even in such an unsettling context. That the *Mickey Mouse Club* anthem, which pervaded television and popular culture in the late 1950s, would still resonate years later is not only a testament to the staying power of the song and the show, but also to the pernicious effects of even the most "innocent" of Cold War televisual symbols.

Jimmie Dodd (upper right) with Mouseketeers on Mickey Mouse Club set

That Cold War context, in particular, will be a significant factor in situating the Detroit experience during the 1950s. The next chapter will consider those historical, political, and social conditions that shaped the cultural landscape that Soupy would occupy during the time that he became a leading television personality in the Motor City.

CHAPTER THREE

THE DETROIT EXPERIENCE IN THE 1950S

Arriving in Detroit in the spring of 1953 to begin his career at WXYZ-TV and his sojourn to becoming a locally well-known television personality, Soupy Hines settled in a duplex on the West Side of the city without his wife and young son (Castelnero 2009: 14). This location on Schaefer Road would provide temporary lodging until his family joined him and they began their journey together from homes in the Jewish neighborhoods on Detroit's West and Northwest areas to the fancy and decidedly non-Jewish suburb of Grosse Pointe. Although close to eighty percent of Jewish families still lived within the Detroit city limits by the late 1950s, many others began their move to nearby suburbs (Berman 2015: 39; and Thompson 2017: 26). Soupy's success by 1958 with a contract that topped $100,000 (an enormous sum that was at least twenty times what the average Detroiter made that year) allowed him to move to a city that was notorious for excluding "racial" and ethnic others.

The discriminatory housing practices in Grosse Pointe would be fully revealed in 1960. (This was the same year that Soupy and his family resided in one of those middling mansions that dotted the tony streets of this suburb. It would also be the last full year that Soupy worked at WXYZ-TV whose studios were no longer in Detroit, but in the nearby suburb of Southfield.) Grosse Pointe realtors relied on an actual "point system" that categorized potential homeowners by race, nationality, occupation, and "degree of swarthiness." In order for Jews, Poles, and Italians to qualify for a house on the market, they required more points than those of the "whiter" ethnics from Northern Europe. Asians and African Americans were not even eligible for consideration. Grosse Pointe homeowners and realtors subsidized the investigation of prospective buyers by private detectives who also reported on "unsavory conduct," such as hanging clothes outdoors. In the aftermath of the revelations about these despicable practices, a state regulatory commission put Grosse Pointe realtors on notice that any discrimination based on race, religion, or national origin would result in the denial of a real estate license (Sugrue 2005: 193).

Nevertheless, the 1950s witnessed much less subtle discriminatory housing practices than a point system, especially when it concerned Black families attempting to move into the "white" areas in the city of Detroit. The same year that Soupy took up residence in Detroit, the Woodsons, an African American family, moved to an all-white neighborhood in the city. They faced a hostile and uninviting reception that came in the form of a letter telling them to "get off this street or we will blow you off." A few days later, someone shot at the front door of their new home. In the aftermath of such threats and actual violence, a spokesman for the local neighborhood association made them an offer they couldn't refuse. Accepting one thousand dollars more than they had paid for the house, the Woodsons fled this inhospitable and potentially deadly environment (Pizzolato 2013: 68). What they experienced in their attempt to become a lone Black family in an all-white neighborhood was replicated throughout Detroit in the 1950s (Johnson 2008: 46; and Sugrue 2005: 209-58).

The striking contrast between what Soupy and his family underwent in their moves around the city and into a suburb and what the Woodsons had to go through is part of the story of the Detroit experience in the 1950s and an important, if often overlooked, aspect of the complicated and contradictory conditions confronted by different families in this period. For Soupy and his family, the Motor City did, indeed, represent a "Mecca" (Sales 2001: 53), the place where he attained fame and success. For many other families, especially African Americans, Detroit was a "mirage," an illusory refuge from discrimination. Providing some background to this institutional discrimination and the resultant struggle against racial injustices in housing and employment will be one of the focal points for this chapter. Moreover, that focus will offer a critical perspective to understanding more fully those contradictions integral to the Detroit experience in the 1950s.

The fight for racial justice during the 1950s was taken up by a number of African American civil rights organizations and activists. One of those prominent activists was Arthur Johnson, the young Executive Director of the Detroit chapter of the NAACP, the largest chapter in the country. Arriving in Detroit in 1950 after completing an undergraduate degree at Morehouse College in Atlanta (graduating in 1948 with Martin Luther King, Jr.) and a Master's Degree from Atlanta University, Johnson was then only twenty-four, a year older than Soupy,

Downtown Woodward Avenue, spine and main shopping venue in 1950s Detroit

Johnson's starting salary was three thousand dollars a year, about one fourth of what Soupy made with his initial contract in 1953, but not much more than the income of thirty percent of Black families at that time. Staying for the first two months at the segregated downtown YMCA, Johnson moved to a Black neighborhood on the West Side of Detroit. While his story does not directly intersect with Soupy's, it, nonetheless, affords a necessary reminder that the Motor City political, socio-economic, and cultural landscape contained inconsistencies that undermined the Detroit boosterism of the times and the golden glow that often accompanies a nostalgic look back at this period.

One of those manufactured memories of the Detroit experience in the 1950s was that this period was one of continual economic advancement for all, especially for those working in the auto industry. In the booming postwar economy, the setbacks for workers and ongoing employment insecurities and discrimination often were hidden in plain sight. Indeed, Detroit's working people, in particular, suffered through four major recessions in the 1950s. In the first half of the 1950s, over one hundred and twenty manufacturing firms relocated to the suburbs while several major auto companies, Hudson and Packard, went out of business (Sugrue 2005: 126-36).

Assembly Line of Plymouth Cars in 1950s Detroit Auto Plant

Certainly, the auto industry did help to create a growing middle class. Nonetheless, this account is complicated by the years of economic insecurity for autoworkers and other members of the working class. While 1953 was a banner year for the auto industry, it was followed by a number of years of recession and economic hardship for autoworkers (Clark 2018). Moreover, employment discrimination in auto and other manufacturing and retail sectors of the Detroit economy meant that workers of color, in particular, faced real adversity (Sugrue 2005: 91-123).

There were others in this era also victimized, not so much by economic conditions or racial injustice as by their political orientations that ran counter to the dominant ideology of the period. Given the Cold War and anti-communist hysteria of the 1950s, political repression was particularly visited upon anyone associated with the political Left. The once prominent Communist Party had to contend with numerous legal and political challenges during this time. Left-wing political activists, as we will see in this chapter, were under constant surveillance. Being watched by antagonistic political forces, the Detroit Police "Red Squad" and the FBI, often led to the loss of jobs and even imprisonment (Pintzuk 1997). Being politically active as a leftist during this period was being consigned to the margins. Yet, it is at those margins that one can see the resonances of a vibrant political and cultural scene even during this period of repression and conformity.

One of those left-wing activists who came to Detroit in 1953, only a few months after Soupy's arrival, was Grace Lee, a highly educated Chinese American who brought more than a decade of radical political experience to the Motor City. (She was to be an incredibly resilient part of this scene until she passed in 2015 at the age of 100.) Soon after she settled in Detroit, she married James Boggs, a Black autoworker and radical, and moved with him to an East Side location that would be a hub of political activity throughout this period and for later decades. Together they would produce a national newspaper and engage in a variety of political activities within and outside their changing organizational affiliations (Lee Boggs 1998; and Ward 2016).

From the WXYZ-TV studios atop the stately Maccabees Building in Midtown Detroit, Soupy could look out at a bustling metropolis. With its peak population in 1950 of over 1.8 million, Detroit laid claim to being the fourth largest city in the United States. Looking south towards the river along the central spine of Woodward Avenue, he might be able to make out the large open spaces of Campus Martius and Grand Circus Park, sites where massive gatherings for political and cultural events would take place, including some for which he later would be master of ceremonies. Also, further downtown, along Woodward, were magnificent movie palaces where Soupy would eventually entertain his youthful fans on Saturday mornings. Nearby to these entertainment venues was the flagship of the retail giant, Hudson's, which drew thousands of Detroiters daily to its enormous consumer emporium. What he might also be able to observe were the thousands and thousands of single family bungalows that radiated out on the West and East Side of the city, inhabited by blue-collar workers and a growing middle class whose kids would become the inveterate viewers of Soupy's noontime program.

What neither he, nor most other whites, could see was that African Americans were excluded from owning those single family homes not only because of discriminatory real estate practices and the prejudices of white neighborhood associations, but also because of governmental policies at a local and national level. Even with the Supreme Court ruling in 1948 in the Shelley versus Kramer case that declared racial covenants unconstitutional, deed restrictions often remained in place, reinforced by realtors, bankers, and white homeowners (Sugrue 2005: 45). As Arthur Johnson recalls in his memoirs, the Supreme Court decision was "on paper...a victory against housing segregation; in practice, however, things were different. Authorities in Detroit (meaning those headed by the racist Mayor Albert Cobo, a conservative Republican who ruled the city from 1950-1957) refused to enforce the Supreme Court decision. Detroit newspapers wrote detailed articles instructing and encouraging white homeowners to circumvent the law and keep blacks out" (Johnson 2008: 43). As a consequence, while private housing units were expanding during the late 40s and early 50s, African Americans, who by the mid-1950s constituted almost a quarter of the population of the city of Detroit, were limited to little more than one to two percent of those units (Sugrue 2005: 43; and Johnson 2008: 45).

The racial discrimination encountered by Detroit Blacks resulted in those segregated neighborhoods where they were mostly confined (like the ironically named "Paradise Valley" on the Lower East Side of the city) becoming hubs of business and cultural activities for African Americans. Johnson remembers the "many evenings (spent) in Paradise Valley enjoying the pulsating energy of Hastings Street and its arteries. Renowned black musicians and entertainers performed in the Valley's clubs and theatres" (Johnson 2008: 50). Nonetheless, even in a place like Paradise Valley, African American residents were threatened with the developing plans of urban renewal that many Blacks saw as "Negro Removal." As a result of freeway designs in the 1950s, urban removal and dislocation especially impacted Black inhabitants of communities like Paradise Valley. One Black resident of the area being cleared for the future Edsel Ford Freeway lamented, "I think it would have been so much nicer to have built places for people to live in than a highway." Such displacement of African Americans continued throughout the 1950s with politicians like Mayor Cobo covering for such policies under the rhetoric of "making progress" (Sugrue 2005: 47-8).

In order to combat those political forces in the city and state that prevented African Americans from finding and affording homes in Detroit neighborhoods previously excluding them, people like Arthur Johnson of the NAACP, the Urban League, and Democratic Party allies, began a political mobilization to enact legislation and engage with intransigent realtors. There were efforts at the state level in 1958 and

1959 to apply "open housing" principles to the real estate market. While those bills promoting "open housing" were defeated, the long march to eliminating housing discrimination would continue with much more success in the 1960s, albeit still fraught with tensions and even violence.

There were other paradoxes that marked the Motor City as a "mirage" when it came to job security. What Soupy could not see from that same vantage point in the Maccabees Building was the beginning of the hemorrhaging of jobs in the Motor City as the Big Three (General Motors, Ford, and Chrysler) began to move some of their factories to the suburbs while automating the jobs once performed by both skilled and unskilled workers. One year after Soupy settled in Detroit, the percentage of automobiles manufactured in Detroit decreased from 35.8 percent to 30.8 percent (Clark 2018: 104). Although there was a slight recovery in 1955, auto dealers were so concerned by another possible economic downtown that they attempted to induce buyers to purchase 1955 models by luring customers with a variety of incentives from new television sets to other appliances, like washing machines and refrigerators, to luxury items like mink coats. More duplicitous sales tactics were often used in order to hook buyers with credit deals. In fact, auto loans during this period totaled half of the U. S. consumer credit (Clark 2018: 125). By 1958, when Soupy had acquired his house in Grosse Pointe, unemployment in Detroit came close to twenty percent of the work force. Many autoworker families had to scuffle to make ends meet, including motivating formerly stay-at-home moms to seek any kind of employment (Clark 2018: 152-56).

The impact on African American autoworkers was even more severe during this period because of racial discrimination in employment and housing. Even at auto factories like the massive Ford Rouge plant in Dearborn, where African American workers achieved a modicum of advancement in the postwar period, the loss of jobs from a total of 85,000 at the end of WWII to around 30,000 in 1960 particularly harmed Black workers who predominated in the ranks of the unskilled. As a consequence of automation and deindustrialization, Black autoworkers faced three times the rate of unemployment as white workers. Especially in the recession of the late 50s, Blacks disproportionately lost jobs at Chrysler where they were a significant percentage of its Motor City workforce (Sugrue 2005: 144 and 162).

As auto factories began the move out of Detroit in the 1950s, African American autoworkers faced other challenges beyond unemployment. Black journalist Charles Wartman, writing in the *Michigan Chronicle* in 1956, predicted the devastating impact that the move to the suburbs by the auto companies would have on its Black workers, especially because of the "housing restrictions" in those suburban cities due to cost and racial biases (Clark 2018: 133). And if Detroit was an inhospitable environment for African Americans seeking employment and housing, the city of Dearborn was worse. The virulently racist Mayor of Dearborn, Orville Hubbard, ran on a platform of keeping Dearborn "lily white." His white constituents manifested their loyalty to him and his platform by constantly re-electing him. (Sugrue 2005: 76).

Employment discrimination and outright segregation of facilities were constant reminders to Black Detroiters throughout the 1950s that they were second-class citizens. Arthur Johnson recounts a wide variety of tactics used by the NAACP to open up restaurants to Black customers and to contest job discrimination in many different fields, including professional occupations in the health industry. Detroit hospitals "refused to train and hire black nurses" with many hospitals having "no black medical professionals" (Johnson 2008: 54). Lawsuits and other legal challenges did little until the passage of the 1964 Civil Rights Act.

Another major area of concern for Arthur Johnson and the Detroit NAACP was the widespread police brutality constantly visited on African Americans by a mostly white Detroit police department. As Johnson recalls, "Over a five-year period between 1956 and 1960, I collected evidence of 149 incidents of police brutality. The beating was so severe in forty-seven of these cases that the black victims required hospitalization" (Johnson 2008: 57). Johnson cites in his memoir several incidents of police brutality. In particular, plainclothes cops continually harassed Black patrons of bars and Black drivers were arrested and thrown in jail on false charges. As he notes, "Offending police officers never admitted to the brutality and were rarely held accountable. In only four cases did the police department admit any wrongdoing on the part of the misbehaving officers" (Johnson 2008: 57).

Although Johnson and the *Michigan Chronicle*, the Detroit-based Black-owned newspaper, documented the incidents of police brutality with accompanying photographs, the main Detroit papers refused to run such stories. When Johnson appeared before the United States Commission on Civil Rights when it came to the Motor City to probe racial matters in December of 1960, he outlined a whole series of changes in police practices that were thought to mitigate police brutality (Johnson 2008: 57-58). (Many of these changes proposed by Johnson, including hiring and promoting more Black cops and training all police on racial matters, would re-emerge in the era of "Black Lives Matter.") Shortly after he testified, Johnson, himself, encountered racist harassment by the Detroit police.

While the egregious actions by Detroit police towards African Americans were a constant throughout the 1950s and beyond, many of those affiliated with left-wing organizations during the height of anti-communist hysteria also faced police repression. When supporters of one progressive civil rights group attended a backyard house party on July 25, 1953, an invading police squad arrested all of those attending the party, charging them with liquor law violations and throwing them in jail overnight. When those charged went to trial before a judge, he publicly denounced them for "meeting as an American front of our enemies when our sons were fighting and dying in Korea" (Babson, *et. al.* 2010: 233).

Native born and naturalized citizens of the United States who were judged by the authorities as being tinged with the "red" virus had to contend with police harassment and legal suppression during the 1950s Red Scare. The leadership of the Michigan Communist Party was indicted by a Grand Jury in 1952 and put on trial (Pintzuk 1997: 158-73). When the Immigration and Nationality Act of 1952 was linked to earlier anti-communist legislation, those undocumented and naturalized citizens suspected of "subversive" activity faced deportation. One of those 10 million naturalized citizens was Stanley Nowak, born in Poland but bred in Michigan and elected repeatedly to the Michigan State Senate. Neither his naturalization nor his political profile protected him from arrest in 1952 and a later trial that resulted in a deportation verdict that the U. S. Supreme Court eventually overruled in 1958 (Babson *et. al.* 2010: 266-73; Pintzuk 1997: 144-47).

Although a fierce Trotskyist critic of the Communist Party, Grace Lee Boggs recalls her introduction to Detroit politics during the Red Scare. Her arrival to Detroit followed shortly after Coleman Young, a left-wing union and civil rights activist, achieved heroic status for standing up to the House Un-American Activities Committee when it met in Detroit in 1952. (Young would first be elected in 1964 to the Michigan State Senate and then in 1973 for five terms as the Mayor of Detroit.) Noting that her husband, James Boggs, worked with "Communists as comrades" in struggles for union and civil rights, she writes in her memoirs, "Like other politically conscious blacks of his generation he recognized that without the Communists it would have taken much longer for blacks to make the leap from being regarded as inferior to being feared as subversive, that is, as a social force" (Lee Boggs 1998: 96).

Her memoirs also render the following first impressions of Detroit as "a city of neighborhoods and beautiful trees. It also felt like a 'Movement' city where radical history had been made and could be made again" (Lee Boggs 1998: 79). This retrospective look at Detroit through the lens of a kind of radical boosterism that informed the last decades of her life stands in contrast to an article written in the 1953 Special Subscription version of the newspaper, *Correspondence*, to which she and James Boggs were attached. The small bi-weekly *Correspondence* advertized itself as "a paper in which ordinary people can say what they want to say and are eager to say" (Ward 2016: 161). Under the heading of "Tension," one of those ordinary people, an African American laborer newly arrived to Detroit, like Grace, provides a more realistic portrayal of the city at the time than the aforementioned version from her the memoir.

"In no other city," writes this anonymous Black worker, "have I felt as much tension as I feel here. The drive to get as much money as possible in as short time as possible (something to which Soupy aspired) is one tension. In the shop in which I work more than a third of the men work two jobs. To get bills paid up. To buy a new car." Continuing to comment on the city's landscape and its creation of "traffic tension," this writer exclaims, "I've never seen a city with so many railroad crossings that cross the main streets. And the railroads seem to use them at the peak of rush hours and further tie up traffic." Ending the article with a reference to tensions in housing and employment for African Americans in particular, the author calls out the "racial tension" as "the most obvious and extreme of all the tensions. It suppresses you on all sides" (in Glaberman papers).

Certainly, both Grace Lee and James Boggs understood that racial tension with all its contradictions. In her memoir, she discusses the impact of the Emmett Till murder in August of 1955 on "Detroit's black community" and its relative "complacency," "It seemed to me that most black Detroiters who had been born and raised in the South were feeling somewhat superior to those who stayed behind, viewing them from the arrogance that city folks often feel toward country folks, seeing them as too backward and apathetic to get up and leave" (Lee Boggs 1998: 105). The shock of the murder of the 13 year-old Till and the acquittal by an all-white Mississippi jury of the two white men who carried out this brutal slaying mobilized the Detroit Black community to attend an NAACP demonstration on September 25, 1955. According to Arthur Johnson, the six thousand attendees constituted "the largest mass demonstration by blacks in Detroit history up until that time" (Johnson 2008: 61-2).

Both Grace and James Boggs were committed to nurturing the insurgencies within the Black community wherever they emerged, even if it put them at odds with the leadership of the NAACP or with their own political organization. A split in their political organization led to a temporary halt in the publication of *Correspondence.* When the paper resumed publishing in 1957, Grace was its editor. Writing under the pseudonym on "Al Whitney," Jimmy urged the small number of readers of the newspaper to go beyond the "expectations" articulated by Dr. Martin Luther King and take up the more militant stance of Robert Williams who preached "self-defense" in his role as the leader of a local NAACP chapter in North Carolina. The revolutions in Africa and Cuba also served as beacons to revolutionary transformation. When the student sit-ins began on February 1, 1960 in Greensboro, North Carolina, Grace penned a preface to a special *Correspondence* edition on those sit-ins, entitled "The First 50 Days – Chronicle of a Revolution." In that preface she wrote, "In years to come historians will tell and re-tell the story of the upheaval we are now living through in the United States" (Ward 2016: 266). Indeed, as numerous historians and sociologists have acknowledged, the 1960s was a historic "decade of disruption" (Morris 1984: 195-228).

While many participated in those disruptions, others, like Soupy Sales, were dealing with their own personal upheavals from changing jobs, moving to different cities, and contending with marital difficulties. Still, Soupy's television shows on WXYZ-TV during the 1950s operated against this backdrop of the Detroit experience, providing a temporary refuge to those upheavals whether through his zany humor or the showcasing of musical talents, both local and national, in particular on his evening show. That show (discussed in more detail in Chapter Five) happily exploited the vibrant cultural scene, especially in the African American community.

As a way of highlighting that cultural scene in the Motor City during the 1950s and to render a more complete picture of Detroit during that period, this chapter will conclude with an examination of the incredibly lively music scene, especially in jazz (Bjorn 2004). Reviewing the jazz clubs and other musical venues from which Soupy drew the performers for his late night show, *Soupy's On*, will help to round out the cultural features of Detroit during this period. It will also offer another way to demarcate the intimate relationship between specific neighborhoods, especially in African American areas of the city, and the kind of musical talent nurtured there that would eventually transform the Motor City into Motown (Maraniss 2016; and Smith 1999).

In looking back on his Detroit experience, Soupy recalled that "One of the great joys of (*Soupy's On*) was that I was able to invite many of the greatest jazz musicians and singers of that era who often passed through Detroit as they toured the country in the mid to late 1950s. These were the halcyon days of jazz, when bop and be-bop were sweeping the nation. Detroit had about twenty-two jazz clubs that you could go to every night of the week and catch somebody good" (Sales 2001: 74). While Soupy's recognition of the impact of Bebop is right on for the nation and Detroit (Stryker 2019: 6-7), his estimation of the number of jazz clubs may be slightly lower than the actual number. Yet, his acknowledgment of the role of those jazz clubs on the Motor City scene and his evening program is both an appropriate conclusion to this chapter and a necessary entry to the discussion in Chapter Five of those jazz performers on his evening show.

Instead of trying to locate the large number of sites where jazz was performed in the 1950s in the Motor City, something that can found in Lars Bjorn and Jim Gallert's excellent book, *Before Motown*, I intend to highlight a number of venues that reflected the vibrant jazz scene and were, most often, the source of those nationally-prominent performers who would appear on *Soupy's On*. Before turning to identifying a handful of those jazz clubs, a brief mention of why there was a proliferation of venues in the 1950s where one could hear jazz, especially the Bebop of that era, is necessary. Even with all the racial discrimination previously discussed, the expanding African American community in Detroit managed to attain a certain level of economic advancement that could support the growth of new businesses like these jazz clubs.

Added to this financial backing was an institutional network in education and religion where music was taught and fully expressed, creating in the process a local stable of jazz performers who could provide entertainment for a variety of Motor City venues. "The city's integrated school system and musicians union...helped cultivate productive relationships between black and white musicians, even as segregation remained in force elsewhere in Detroit" (Stryker 2019: xii). Music education programs at a number of key Detroit high schools, such as Cass Tech and Northern High, reflected the connections between that institutional context and the development of jazz artists like Sheila Jordan, Doug Watkins, Donald Byrd, Paul Chambers, Tommy Flanagan, and Roland Hanna (Macias 2010: 52). Many of these and other Detroit jazz musicians (cited below) would go one to become some of the nationally recognized "young lions" of modern jazz (Stryker 2019: 44-72).

One of the jazz clubs that first emerged as the place for modern jazz was the Blue Bird Inn. Located on the northern edge of the West Side Black community, the Blue Bird Inn was a hangout for young Detroit musicians who would later gain national prominence. The Blue Bird Inn was especially important for the development of Detroit great native pianists of that era. As recalled by one of those pianists, Barry Harris, the Blue Bird Inn was "the joint I would run to when I was too young to get in...My twenty-first birthday was celebrated in the Blue Bird to make sure they knew I was twenty one" (Bjorn 2001: 100). Tommy Flanagan, another Detroit born-and-bred legendary pianist, described the Blue Bird Inn as "a beautiful club...I never saw a place like it even in New York. It had a neighborhood atmosphere and all the support a jazz club needed" (Bjorn2004: 165; and Macias 2010: 49).

Clarence Eddins, one of a number of African American owners and managers of Motor City jazz venues, not only expanded the size of the venue in the late 1950s, he also contracted with some of the leading Bebop musicians, from Art Blakey's Jazz Messengers to the Horace Silver Quintet to the Miles Davis Sextet (Bjorn 2001: 117).

But it was also the house band at the Blue Bird Inn that often even intimidated these better-known jazz performers. As pianist and Detroit native, Bess Bonnier, remembered about one of the local jazz aggregations there, "The Thad Jones-Billy Mitchell quintet was the best group at the Blue Bird Inn. It was world class, and Thaddeus (the trumpet player) was not to be believed." According to Roland Hanna, another amazing Detroit jazz pianist who saw Thad Jones at the Blue Bird and took note of how he impressed others: "There was only one other person who was his equal and that was Dizzy. Miles (Davis) would stand under the air conditioner with tears running out of his eyes when he heard Thad play" (Bjorn 2001: 130).

Joe Henderson Quartet on the Blue Bird Inn stage in the late 1950s

Starting in late 1953 and through the first several months of 1954, Miles came to Detroit to try to kick his heroin habit. He would occasionally join the house band at the Blue Bird Inn during this time (Stryker 2019: 161). His own recollection of who also appeared at the Blue Bird is another testament to the draw that club had for the local jazz scene as it later transferred to the national stage. "I had been playing the Blue Bird for several months as a soloist – a guest soloist – in Billy Mitchell's house band. The band also had Tommy Flanagan on piano and Elvin Jones on drums. Betty Carter (the amazing vocalist) used to come and sit in with Yusef Lateef (multi-reed instrumentalist), Barry Harris, Curtis Fuller (trombonist), and Donald Byrd (trumpeter). It was a real hip city for music" (Davis 2011: 173). Davis was right about how hip the city was for music. He would return again and again to Detroit to play at the Blue Bird Inn in the late 1950s and other jazz venues. During those gigs in Detroit, he would also appear as a guest soloist on *Soupy's On* (more on this in Chapter Five).

In his memoir, Miles refers to performing during his Detroit residency at another jazz club, Baker's Keyboard Lounge (Davis 2011: 173-74; and Bjorn 2001: 134). Unlike most of the other venues that were located on the West and East side of the center city, Baker's was on the edge of the northern city limits. Although jazz had been performed there since the 1930s, Baker's only began to feature national acts in the mid-1950s (Bjorn 2001: 117). During that period, however, the caravan of jazz musicians who played at Baker's was truly astounding. The following list makes it clear that this particular club was the place to see the jazz luminaries of the period. These included the Clifford Brown/Max Roach Quintet, Art Tatum, Erroll Garner, Dave Brubeck, Oscar Peterson, Anita O'Day, Gerry Mulligan, and Ahmad Jamal (originally Fritzie Jones from Pittsburgh). Although many of these performers also appeared at other venues throughout the city, Baker's had a special arrangement with Soupy's evening program on WXYZ-TV, *Soupy's On*. In exchange for promoting Baker's on the show, artists performing there would be contractually required to appear as a musical guest on *Soupy's On* at some point during their gig at the club (Sales 2001: 77).

Clifford Brown's appearance on *Soupy's On* either months or weeks before he died in a tragic car crash in June 1956 at the incredibly young age of 25 was during a gig at another jazz club also on the edge of the city. The Rouge Lounge, where the Clifford Brown/Max Roach Quintet performed twice in 1956, was actually over the Detroit border on the Southwest Side in the working class community of River Rouge, a community that would become majority Black by the end of the 1950s. The owners and managers of the club, Tom and Ed Sarkesian, recruited jazz greats like Charlie Parker, Roy Eldridge, Ben Webster, Johnny Hodges, and Billie Holiday to perform at the club from 1953 until the late 1950s. (All of the aforementioned would become guests on *Soupy's On*.) Ed Sarkesian also produced national jazz concert tours, including pulling together an "American Jazz Festival" at the Michigan State Fair Grounds in Detroit in 1959 that lasted only for one year more. However, that festival not only demonstrated the appeal of Detroit as a major jazz venue, but also awed jazz journalists like *Downbeat's* Ira Gitler with the excellence of the performances by local musicians (Bjorn 2001: 119-20).

Among the jazz venues that nurtured those local musicians was the Crystal Show Bar, situated on the near West Side. In 1951, the Crystal gained a local following as an integrated "black and tan" club. Taking note of this move, the *Detroit Tribune* wrote, "The Crystal Bar, one of

Detroit's two new inter-racial nightclubs, this week appeared ready to switch from the sweet song, piano-playing entertainment to rousing, jumping combo music." Among the rousing performances at the Crystal were several engagements by Charlie Parker in 1954. Working with local musicians for his back-up rhythm section, Parker put on two especially memorable shows. During this time he also appeared on *Soupy's On* (Bjorn 2001: 113-14. Additional discussion of this appearance will be covered in Chapter Five). Among other jazz artists who worked the Crystal Show Bar during the 1950s were Lester Young and, again, Miles Davis.

Another Show Bar, the Flame, was located on a street, John R, in the midtown area of the Near East Side that had so many different clubs, including jazz venues, that it was called the "Street of Music." The owner, Morris Wasserman, one of several prominent Jewish jazz club proprietors during this period, promoted the Flame Show Bar as a "black and tan." One of the members of the house band, Maurice King's Wolverines, recalls that the scene "there was just poppin.' Lights and glitter, valet parking...White people would come from all over to come to the Flame, because we had the top shows" (Bjorn 2001: 72). King's Wolverines consisted of local musicians who were flexible enough to play both jazz and rhythm and blues. While jazz performers like Billie Holiday and Louis Jordan of "Jump Jazz" fame played the Flame, the R & B singers, from Johnnie Ray and LaVern Baker to Della Reese and Jackie Wilson, not only graced the stage there but also went on to record some of the early hits of popular music in the 1950s.

Although there were some minor labels recording these and other Detroit popular musicians, the lack of a major record label in town (pre-Motown) led many of the Motor City jazz musicians to move to New York City or Los Angeles in the late 1950s. By 1960 the music scene for jazz performers in Detroit became even more limited as the number of jazz clubs declined (Macias 2010: 57). With the additional impact of an economic recession and strikes in auto and steel, the ability of making a living in the local club scene was very constrained. Those Detroit musicians who left the city, nonetheless, took with them what Hank Jones labeled "the Detroit drive, the Motor City drive" (Macias 2010: 65). As jazz critic Leonard Feather would comment in his liner notes to a Blue Note album called, *Detroit-New York Junction*, "the title...signifies a happy marriage between the rapidly growing musical produce of the Motor City and the magnetic tape of the Big Apple" (Bjorn 2001: 64).

The allure of the Big Apple would eventually bring Soupy Sales, along with the cohort of Detroit jazz artists, to New York City in the early 1960s. Of course, like them, he sharpened his skills, albeit comedic, in Detroit during the 1950s. The next chapter will consider how Soupy Sales developed those talents as a daytime children's television personality.

CHAPTER FOUR

SOUPY'S DAYTIME TV SHOWS

WXYZ-TV, the ABC affiliate in Detroit, had been in operation for almost five years when Soupy, known only by his first name for several months, appeared as a new face at noontime in the spring of 1953. While the show, *12 O'Clock Comics*, was relatively innovative because of its content and time slot, the television station actually had been one of the first in the country to have regular programming during the afternoon hours (Osgood 1981: 262-64). The WXYZ-TV general manager, John Pival, had conceived of a half-hour show that would consist of a mixture of cartoons and slapstick silent films with a live host to entertain children and share lunch with them. When Pival selected Soupy for the job of host, it kicked-off a daytime career as a madcap lunchtime buddy to kids that would run from 1953 to 1960, manufacturing in the process a wildly popular television personality in Detroit. At its inception, however, one of the other employees at the station believed that "Pival had made a terrible mistake. Here was this kid who was zany...but was just a kid. In about a week or two we realized we had a real comic genius" (Castelnero 2009: 30). That comic genius helped to create one of the most loved and successful children's television show in the Motor City.

On the other hand, Soupy could not lay claim to being the first popular children's program on a Detroit television station. Preceding Soupy by almost three years on a rival network, WJBK-TV, was a white-faced clown in an all white costume. "Milky the Clown," so designated as a way of linking him to the Twin Pines Dairy Company, the sponsor of the Saturday afternoon show, quickly attracted a young audience. As one of those viewers later recalled, "Milky was probably the most popular clown in Detroit – everyone knew him. What was unusual about him was that you never saw a clown that was all white before; the white suit and the white facial makeup really made him unique" (Castelnero 2006: 81-2). Although Milky's look with "the pointed hat" and "the all-white suit" may have struck some viewers as having a sinister resemblance to the KKK, the image "was much more about the milk theme and patterning it after the classic opera clown, Pagliacci" (Castelnero 2006: 86).

Instead of an outlandish costume, like Milky, Soupy materialized on daytime television without the exaggerated trappings of a clown. "Though he was every bit the clown that Clarabell was (one of the characters on the *Howdy Doody Show*, another very popular daytime television program for kids during the 1950s), or, the character that Pinky Lee played, Sales rejected the notion of wearing any additional costume" (Grossman 1987: 127). What he did wear would become his regular outfit. According to Soupy, it was the station's "idea for me to wear a ridiculous top hat, an oversized bow tie, and a black sweater" (Sales 2001: 54). Thus, Soupy's outfit became his TV costume and its individual components marked him whenever he would appear at public gatherings where kids predominated.

As far as the show's set and production, Soupy played a major role in designing both. "The set was supposed to be a representation of my house, kind of like Soupy's clubhouse, and I would be sitting at a table with a checkered tablecloth, and I'd be having lunch" (Sales 2001: 58). Hence, the sense of ordinariness and familiarity built into the set. Soupy's demeanor on the show also offered the kind of intimacy integral to the manufacturing of a television personality (Bennett 2011: 26-34). Jack Flechsig, the WXYZ-TV art director recalls Soupy having a "very clear idea of what he wanted, what he required in the way of a set. I merely embellished what he described he wanted. He needed a door in the middle of the set to do bits with, and he needed a window...a lone window for puppets to appear in...and he needed a wall...He would always have me making pictures on the wall that became animated. One of them was a picture of a crying baby...and the baby would be crying, crying, crying, and he would finally get annoyed and go over and turn the picture over and it would be the backside of the baby showing" (Castelnero 2009: 19-20).

The wall was also the site for a blackboard upon which were written two different kinds of messages. On occasion, there would be "Words of Wisdom," Soupy's prosaic lessons, an example of which would be "People who eat sweets take up two seats." One fan of the show remembers that after Soupy would read the "Words of Wisdom," he would ask "what do we mean by that?" to be answered off-camera by a voice that would repeat, "Yeah, what do we mean by that?" "And after explaining what the words meant, and what you should do (because there was always a real-life lesson to be learned), Soupy would look at you and say, 'You do dat, I love you and give you a big kiss" (Sales 2001: 69). At other times the blackboard contained those corny jokes that came under the heading of "Soupy Sez." A case in point was the following: "Show me a toilet in a castle and I'll show you a royal flush" (Sales 2001: 68 and 67).

Although Soupy's clubhouse was hardly a castle, it was flush with amazing characters that soon endeared themselves to his growing audience. Among the most improbable and memorable characters were two dogs, White Fang and Black Tooth. Bill Carruthers, one of the directors on *Lunch with Soupy Sales*, reminisced about "this imagery of two huge dogs, represented by two paws that came into range of the black-and-white camera from the left and right frame, with these two very distinct voices" (Sales 2001: 59). (Every single person among the two dozen I interviewed identified these two when asked which characters they remembered from Soupy's lunchtime show.) A woolly white paw and a low growling weird voice were the trademarks of White Fang, "the meanest dog in the world," or, in "Dee-troit." On the other hand, a furry brown paw and high-pitched voice were the markers of Black Tooth, "the sweetest dog in the world," or, in "Dee-troit," who was always kissing and slobbering over Soupy (Sales 2001: 60).

Both White Fang and Black Tooth were inventions that Soupy and Clyde Adler, a stage manager and director at WXYZ-TV, built into the daily bits on the show. Tim Kiska, a Detroit television critic, labeled Adler "local television's greatest unseen force" (Kiska 2005: 5). While never on camera, Adler added immensely to the appeal of the show. In addition, Adler and Soupy shared a number of interesting connections. Adler's family lived in Grosse Pointe where he graduated from high school in 1944 and then entered the U. S. Navy during World War II. After attending Michigan State University, on the G.I. Bill that millions of other veterans, like Soupy, took advantage of, Adler was hired by WXYZ-TV. It was in that capacity that he and Soupy hooked up for the noontime children's program. According to another producer who worked on the program during this time, Adler was "the workhorse of that show. It was like Dean Martin and Jerry Lewis – they worked on each other" (Kiska 2001). That rapport between Clyde and Soupy was, for the most part, ad-lib. As his widowed wife, Jane Adler, recalls, even though Clyde's personality was more restrained than Soupy, White Fang provided Clyde with an outlet for expressing a more freewheeling character.

Soupy with Clyde Adler as White Fang on the WXYZ TV set

There were times, however, when Frank Nastasi filled in for Adler. Nastasi was a working actor in Detroit who appeared on another WXYZ-TV children's program, *Wixie's Wonderland*. Taking over when Adler went on vacation, Nastasi added a different intonation and voicing for White Fang, as well as performing other roles. "We used to break up on the show," Nastasi recalls. "And that was part of the charm....The way it usually worked was like this: We had a short meeting before the show. Soupy would say, 'All right Frank, you do this and you do this.' I'll take this punch line and you take that punch line...We ad-libbed and filled in all around the punch lines" (Sales 2001: 65-6). Such free-style comedic banter helped enable the sense of spontaneity and authenticity pervading the show, reinforcing in the process the manufacturing of Soupy as a television personality.

Whoever had the punch line, it was usually White Fang, whether executed by Clyde Adler or Frank Nastasi, who caused trouble for Soupy. In that regard and from the perspective of Jewish humor, White Fang was the schlemiel to Soupy's schlimazel. (The definition for the Yiddish meaning of schlemiel is the one who spills the soup and the schlimazel is the one upon whom the soup is spilled.) For example, in one of the few excerpts of the WXYZ-TV production of *Lunch with Soupy Sales* that can be found on YouTube, Soupy scolds

White Fang for trying to read in the dark. So, White Fang takes out a light bulb and proceeds to hook it up to Soupy's head. When White Fang pulls the chord, the blinding light (exaggerated even more by a close-up camera shot) is too much for Soupy who turns it off. Immediately, the big paw shoots out, pulls the chord, and grabs a newspaper to shove in front of Soupy and the light bulb. While White Fang reads aloud with his unintelligible, but humorous, "Reh-O-Reh-Oh," Soupy stands there like a schlimazel, someone on whom a joke has been played.

The joke, of course, relies on a number of psychological mechanisms that are triggered in the brain, especially, but not exclusively, in developing children. First and foremost, there are known cognitive connections to what is called the incongruity factor in humor. Without going too deeply into the neuroscience of this incongruity factor, there is a portion of the brain that is particularly responsive to releases from reality and challenges to what is imagined to be real (McGhee 1972: 77; and Neely *et.al.* 2012: 1788-89). That there could be a dog of that size, represented by a large white paw and bizarre non-barking dog sounds that only Soupy, as the straight man, vaudevillian interlocutor, and/or schlimazel, can interpret, certainly adheres to this incongruity factor. In addition, the make-believe part of having this kind of exchange between a supposed dog and man conforms to how joking as a form of "pretend play" invents "fictitious deformations of the world" that cause children to find humor in such exchanges (Bariaud 1988: 18-22). As a critical component of incongruity, playfulness inheres in humor that extends beyond childhood. Indeed, incongruity is a central factor in humor for all ages (Palmer 1994: 93-110).

Another example of incongruity involves an exchange between White Fang and Soupy and a third party, the infamous "angry neighbor" who appears as a hand and loud voice when the clubhouse door is opened. (Sometimes that angry neighbor, yelling about Soupy's dogs invading his shrubbery, officially answers to "the-man-at-the-door.") In one of the only full episodes that still can be seen on YouTube from the nationally syndicated Saturday show, *Lunch with Soupy Sales* (the one that I saw in October of 1959), White Fang grabs a whistle from Soupy and begins blowing it. Already there is incongruity because, instead of a man blowing a dog whistle, there is a dog blowing a noisy regular whistle. The added element occurs when there is a knock on the door with the outstretched hand gesticulating and complaining about the loudness of the blown whistle while he is trying to get some sleep. Soupy promises the neighbor that his sleep will not be disturbed again, only to be confounded when White Fang continues making those shrill sounds. After a few rounds of this, Soupy grabs the whistle away from White Fang. Going to the door once more, Soupy is confronted by the hand, an angry voice, and then pulled off camera to return with the whistle shoved in his mouth.

Certainly, there are elements of humor as the release of aggression in the above example of the angry neighbor that can appeal to both kids and adults. What is intriguing about this and other examples of discord at the door from the next-door neighbor is that it contradicts the tendency of children's television during the 1950s to produce and promote domestic tranquility. While the angry neighbor bits hardly represented the levels of labor and racial conflict in Detroit during the 1950s, the comedic displacement through these slapstick routines on Soupy's noontime show did reflect some level of trouble in the neighborhood that often resulted in Soupy being the recipient of some minor aggressive act.

There are less belligerent, but no less humorous, exchanges between Soupy and someone at the door. In this same aforementioned episode of the noontime show, there is another knock on the door. This time the off-screen person, identifying himself as a deliveryman for the "Inky Dinky Toy Shop," gives a package to Soupy for which Soupy pays one dollar. When Soupy asks for his change of half a buck, he is presented with the head of a deer. Of course, needing to have some sense of the referents involved, namely "half a buck" for fifty cents and deer and buck as interchangeable names, provides the humor here, especially in its distortion of the meaning of "half a buck." Thus, as the child psychologist, Francoise Bariaud, explains, "humor requires possession of the referents it distorts" (Bariaud 1988: 24). This is evident in another exchange between Soupy and the man at the door, sometimes also referred to as the "Nut-at-the-Door." In this incident, Soupy is confronted by the voice asking: "What would you do if you were in my shoes?" Soupy, looking down, makes a funny face and responds, "I'd polish them." The joke then gets turned back on Soupy when he gets hit with a pie (Sales 2001: 58). Some unwanted resolution for Soupy, but a funny release for those watching, reinforcing Mel Brooks's distinction between tragedy and comedy. Tragedy for Brooks is when he falls down an open manhole; comedy is when someone else does.

For Soupy and his studio crew, there was a less harrowing but still hilarious meaning for the kind of comedy practiced on the daytime show. Soupy's own definition of what was funny – "a person falls down and gets up" – epitomized both the conscious gags on the show and the spontaneous pranks that broke up both Soupy and the stagehands. As Bill Carruthers noted, "The audience for the show was basically the crew, and Soupy related to the crew. We had guys behind the camera laughing. Stagehands (were) our audience...Make them laugh, and you've really got something. He never knew what we were going to do and we never knew what he was going to do" (Sales 2001: 60). Among the practical jokes the stagehands perpetrated on Soupy was putting brandy, instead of apple juice, in his glass or vodka is his orange juice. Screwed by the stagehands with a screwdriver concoction, a startled Soupy, however, stayed in character, exclaiming "Mmm, boy, that's good." Another time there was a mix-up with the sound operator, leading to a knock on the door with the unexpected yell – "'WHY DON'T YOU SHUT UP!" (Castelnero 2009: 24-5). Soupy doubled over with laughter, surprised by what he heard, but nowhere near as surprised as he was on another episode when he saw a naked lady at the door.

One of the cameramen recounts what transpired during that notorious incident: "We're doing the show as normal, and the director, Bill Carruthers, said 'Go behind the set and get the shots when they come up.' I had no idea what the shots were gonna be...My camera's sitting there, and here comes this young lady with a robe on. She wanders back, stands behind the door, then proceeds to take her robe off...she has nothing on but high heels. And she's preening and primping herself for when he opens the door...When Soupy opened the door, she just stood there and posed. It was a definite surprise," especially because Soupy thought it was live on the air (Castelnero 2009: 26). Fortunately for the television station, it was only the male gaze of Soupy and the crew that ogled the naked lady instead of the show's audience.

The knock at the door did not always result in Soupy being fooled or surprised by the crew or getting hit with a pie. "Sometimes if there was a commotion outside and Soupy went to investigate," writes Gordon Castelnero, "the viewers would catch a glimpse of a ridiculous film clip. Snippets containing celluloid images of such loony scenarios as a man pulling an elephant or circus acrobats on trapezes were inserted to give the illusion that nothing but utter nonsense managed to find its way to Soupy's house" (Castelnero 2009: 21). After introducing himself with his patented "Soupy Shuffle," the Saturday show, *Lunch with Soupy Sales*, opens with a knock at the door and a man claiming that his dancing chicken, Clarissa, is a better dancer than Soupy. Cut to a ridiculous cinematic shot of a scratching chicken in apparent dance mode that Soupy says is no big deal. As an answer to his pooh-poohing the dancing chicken, there is a cacophony of clucking that produces larger and larger eggs, as if to say "try doing this."

More often than not, however, the knock on the door resulted in Soupy having a pie thrown in his face. One example of the set-up for the thrown pie is the following gag routine:

> There's a knock at the door and a traveling psychiatrist arrives in answer to Soupy's desperate telephone plea for help.
> Soupy: "Ya gotta tell me, doc, is it possible for a man to be in love with an elephant?"
> Psychiatrist, using Viennese accent: "No, it is not possible? A man cannot be in love with an elephant!"
> Soupy: (Whipping out a piece of jewelry the size of a hula-hoop): "In that case, do you know where I can get rid of an engagement ring this big?"
> A pie comes out of nowhere, hitting Soupy in the face. (Sales 2001: 72)

The humor inherent in pie-in-the-face gags (a staple of Soupy's television personality) is further reinforced in the variety of slapstick sprinkled throughout Soupy's shows, especially in the showing of silent comedy films. In the movie shown for the Saturday premier of *Lunch with Soupy Sales*, both the vaudevillian craziness and pratfalls and Soupy's pun-driven voice-over rely on certain kinds of humor. "Slapstick comedy in particular," as maintained by a team of neuroscientists, "does not require the same frontal cortex-powered problem solving and integration of content requisite of appreciating more nuanced forms of humor" (Neely, et. al. 2012: 1789). The various slapstick routines performed by Soupy and on the old-time silent films certainly weren't nuanced. Getting hit in the face with a flying fish in one incident in the silent film and knocked about in another depends on slapstick routines that were made even more outrageous by the visual tricks of the early silent films.

While younger children may laugh at these incidents, Soupy's wordplay jokes require a more sophisticated cognitive development. (For some adults, there is no "sophistication" needed for appreciating or, indeed, tolerating puns even though great writers like Shakespeare and Melville deployed them.) In the case of his narrative for the movie, Soupy makes several puns including referring to the flying sailfish as "on sale for $3.98." Of course, if you know there is such a thing as a sailfish and understand implicitly at a basic level how homonyms work, the pun is funnier.

Soupy's humor, thus, could operate on a number of levels, depending on whether it was straight slapstick comedy or wordplay. According to Ed Golick, the webmaster of *Detroitkidshow.com*: "He would do some material that kind of went over the heads of little kids. First he had little kids watching, and then the teenage kids kind of got hooked on it. He did things on about two or three different levels for the little kids and the teenagers, and then the adults started watching the thing" (Castelnero 2009: 23). While the silent films might work with older kids and adults because of Soupy's voice-over gag and pun filled narration, the puppets, especially those that accompanied Soupy when he sat down to lunch had an immediate appeal to younger kids.

One of those loveable little puppets was Pookie the Lion. A small puppet that appeared at the window by Soupy's lunchtime table, Pookie was first performed by Clyde Adler without a voice although definitely conveying, in the words of Jane Adler, a "snarky tone." (According to Jane, Clyde handled Pookie and the other puppets with such aplomb that he was later asked to join the Jim Henson muppets crew. Given some of his own health issues, Clyde had to decline the offer.) Later, Frank Nastasi added a voice to Pookie, often referring to Soupy as "booby" (Sales 2001: 64).

While Pookie's name came from Soupy's nickname for his eldest son Tony, the puppet's design was originally attributed to the puppeteer, Bil Baird. Because of the fear of copyright infringement from Baird, Soupy had another puppet created that looked similar but with enough minor changes to avoid any legal issue (Castelnero 2009: 17-18).

Regardless of who handled the puppet, Pookie would mostly pantomime to records in order to suggest different voices and situations for the exchange between Soupy and the hand puppet. One example is when Soupy starts reading about "Little Bo-Peep who has lost her sheep and doesn't know where to find them." The recorded response is "Well, that's reasonable, isn't it. It's reasonable to assume if Little Bo Peep has lost her sheep, it's only natural that she wouldn't know where to find them" (Sales 2001: 57). More often, Pookie and Soupy would re-enact a parodied song. In the aforementioned Saturday show, Soupy takes a toy drum as Pookie mimes the 1955

Stan Freberg version of "The Yellow Rose of Texas." In this Freberg parody, the drummer, in this case Soupy, drowns out the lyrics, causing the singer, Freberg/Pookie, to denounce the drummer as a Yankee-loving disrupter of the of the song. (Freberg recorded other parodies of hit pop tunes of the 1950s, such as "The Great Pretender" and the "Rock Island Line," along with original sketch comedic audio bits for Capitol Records, like "John and Marsha." The latter corresponded somewhat to certain Sid Caesar routines, the kind, also, that Soupy would do on his evening program.)

Soupy at Lunch with Pookie on WXYZ TV set

It's obvious from the sort of gags and routines that Soupy performed on his noontime show that not only children would be attracted as viewers. As Soupy asserts, "I knew my kind of humor appealed to adults and to kids. I never talked down to the kids; I interacted with them, the same way I would interact with adults. After all, I was nothing more than a king-sized kid myself. And I think the kids understood and really dug that. But once I found out that adults were watching, too. I never consciously changed anything to play to them" (Sales 2001: 61). As one mom observed in a letter to the *Detroit Free Press* about the reaction to Soupy's show by her and her kids: "He has become their idol and they love him and look up to him. Sometimes the only laugh I get out of a day is when I happen to catch some of his program" (3/18/1956: 37). It is probably not too much of an exaggeration when Dick Clark claims, "Soupy grabbed an audience of the very young, their moms and dads and teens. That's almost impossible to do. He became everybody's 'guy'" (Sales 2001: 68)

In order to become everybody's "guy," Soupy generated a sense of identification and a feeling of intimacy with him. The connection that Soupy cultivated with his audience was that he "was one of them, the little guy who was sometimes overwhelmed with life, but who somehow always managed to get through it" (Sales 2001: 60). The intimacy that Soupy consciously manufactured and nurtured was speaking directly to the audience through the use of close-ups and breaking the so-called fourth wall. "Though he never spoke my name," Ed Golick recollects, "I knew that Soupy was talking just to me from that TV screen" (Kiska 2001). From Soupy's perspective: "I wanted it to seem as if I were right in the room with them, that I really was part of their family" (Sales 2001: 61). Such intimacy, as noted previously, was not only a hallmark of the show, but also a key component for manufacturing Soupy as a television personality (Bennett 2011: 32-34).

The early audience reaction to the show, as reported in various stories and letters in the *Detroit Free Press* during the first year and a half, attests to the family appeal that Soupy's television personality conveyed. In a letter that appeared in the "Prevue's" mailbag column on June 24, 1954, Soupy gets praised for how "he teaches kids good safety rules and good manners (123). (The same can't be said of White Fang's example.) Soupy did have his detractors, as can be seen from a letter in the *Free Press* that called him "dull" and viewed him as little more than a "jumping jack" (1/10/1954). However, the overwhelming response from the letters he received each week and those that appeared in print was positive, if not downright laudatory. One of those admiring letters in the *Free Press* came from a recent arrival to Detroit from New York City. The letter writer laments that NYC "never had such a delightful show as Soupy Sales has...His sparkling personality plus the well-constructed programming provides a half hour each noon of fun for young and old" (6/27/54: 13). However, another letter-writer admonishes Soupy that he might be forgetting that his "viewers are pre-school age and half-day kindergarten children. Keep it simple, less talking, more cartoons" (*Free Press* 6/13/54: 48).

Interestingly, in its initial advertising, WXYZ-TV promoted that family connection for the *12 O'Clock Comics*. An April 2, 1953 ad in the *Detroit Free Press* in the so-called "Women's Section" of the newspaper encouraged moms to turn to WXYZ-TV at noontime by emphasizing "Your youngsters will eat a good lunch for sure when they watch "Soupy" on the *12 O'Clock Comics*." The ad continued to run for over a month in that same section, inducing mothers and kids to have their lunch with Soupy. That pitch for having lunch with Soupy caught on as confirmed by a growing audience that deluged him with nearly one thousand letters a week (*Free Press* 5/16/54: 55). In addition, there was a near unanimous acknowledgement among my interviewees that they would eat their lunch with Soupy. Another person remembers "myself and probably other kids would run home from school to watch the show. It was like being in his house...he had a table, and that's where lunch would be served." Kids would implore their mothers, in particular, to prepare their lunches following the menus advertised on the show. "I would just say to my mom," recalls Peggy Tibbits, 'Tomorrow I want to have tomato soup and a grilled cheese sandwich.' And I would want to eat on a TV tray and watch Soupy Sales when I came home" (Castelnero 2009: 11-12).

This dynamic required both stay-at-home moms and a long lunchtime recess from a nearby school, something that began to change by the end of the 1950s. As Dick Osgood wrote in his column in the *Detroit Free Press* on June 7, 1953 "Soupy usually warns mothers the day before what to have ready the next noon" (50), Reinforcing the lunchtime rituals and menus meant that Soupy would become, as he later noted, "responsible for shaping the eating habits of thousands of Detroit kids" (Sales 2001: 56). He acknowledged that "we had the approval of some group that was cognizant of lunches, and we figured as long as we had milk and basic things it was okay" (Castlenero 2009: 15). There were even appeals in the newspaper with Soupy's face encouraging "you nice bird baths" (Soupy's made-up designation for his young audience that eventually become the name of his fan club) to join him at noon on Channel 7 for "lunch and more comedy movies" (*Free Press* May 5, 1953: 29). The ads for the show eventually moved in June 1953 to the "Comics" section of the newspaper and then to the television page where one could see the banner line – "Hey Kids! –

Hurry home from school to watch Soupy each weekday at 12 noon" (*Detroit Free Press*, 9/15/1953: 33).

A specific sponsor or an announcement of an upcoming public appearance often accompanied the newspaper ads, making the commercial connections, especially to the food industry, very evident. National Food Stores was the sponsor of the aforementioned ad, urging kids to "hurry home" at lunch. The *Detroit Free Press* of June 14, 1953 contained a note about Soupy's live telecast from Wrigley's Supermarket. Like so many of the television programs in the Motor City and around the country, the large companies in the food industry, like General Foods, dominated the sponsorship of kids' shows. In fact, Jell-O, a General Foods brand, was the sponsor for Soupy's nationally syndicated *Lunch with Soupy Sales* that first aired on October 3, 1959. Not only would Soupy be serving up "a double helping of smiles, giggles, and laughs," as expressed in a *Free Press* ad (10/17/1959: 23), but also Soupy would devote an inordinate amount of time on the show to promote Jell-O. As he later recalled, "I sold a hell of a lot of Jell-O well before Bill Cosby tasted his first spoonful on TV" (Sales 2001: 83).

In that premier of the ABC syndicated Saturday noontime show, Soupy enlisted the aid of White Fang and Black Tooth to sell Jell-O to his audience. The pitch for purchasing Jell-O was, of course, part of the lunch that Soupy ate. Biting from a hot-dog that growled like a dog and drinking milk accompanied by a "mooing" sound, Soupy finished off his lunch with a desert of ice cream with Jell-O sprinkled on top. The references to Jell-O (encompassing up to eight full minutes during the half hour program) were also sprinkled throughout the show. The knock-on-the-door included a baby's hand grabbing Soupy's box of Jell-O. The most absurd bit, however, and one that may have not been to the sponsor's liking, was when White Fang began throwing the contents of one of the Jell-O boxes in the air, leading Soupy to open an umbrella to protect him from Jell-O downpour. As Soupy might say in another context -"If you let a smile be your umbrella, you're liable to get a face full of rain" - or, in this case, a face full of Jell-O flakes through the shenanigans of White Fang. White Fang's tomfoolery, in this instance, subverted the pitch to purchase Jell-O for its specific merchandizing function as a commodity for consumption.

Being a pitchman for Jell-O on his noontime show reflected the fact that many locally produced television programs in the 1950s built-in their single-sponsored ads for promotion by the host of the show (McAllister and Giglio 2005: 29). As Soupy recalls in his memoir: "In those days...things were pretty free and easy insofar as commercials were concerned. We knew what we had to say about the product, but there were no time constraints. Many of the commercials ran two, three, sometimes four minutes, and we'd just ad-lib like crazy, using whatever happened to be at hand" (Sales 2001: 83). Those ad-libs, in particular when involving the incongruous role of White Fang as a slapstick interlocutor, might have enhanced the comedic quality of the commercial while potentially undermining the more somber pitch to consume the sponsored product.

The balance between promoting a product like Jell-O and keeping up the madcap pace for gags and comedy bits, therefore, was an intricate dance. As Soupy observes, "Our shows were not actually written, but they were precisely thought out until the point where we knew we had to get into a commercial. But the greatest thing about the show, and I think the reason for its success, was that it seemed undisciplined. When you get right down to it, its was extremely disciplined. The more you can make a performance seem spontaneous, the better entertainer you are" (Sales 2001: 59). The spontaneity, whether contrived or not, was a compelling attraction to my friends and me. The contrast with practically all other children's shows seemed to make Soupy and his cast more authentic and less programmed, more madcap and less constrained.

Yet, when Soupy got the call to replace the popular children's show, *Kukla, Fran and Ollie*, for a two-month summer run from July 4 to August 6, 1955, there was a larger crew with a more targeted focus. As reported in the *Free Press* on June 12, 1955, "The new series, designed for a juvenile audience, will be produced without scripts. Peter Strand, who has produced Soupy's local shows, will work out the 'story line' with Sales for the network series" (Osgood, 50). The "story line" entailed an obvious attempt to provide some coherence to the daily program, especially since it would air live from Detroit at 6 p.m. John Riddell, the WXYZ President, observed that the show would be "the first regularly scheduled commercial network TV show to originate in Detroit" (Osgood, 50). As a consequence, the city of Detroit issued a proclamation congratulating "Soupy's step into national television" (*Detroit Free Press*, 7/3/1995: 31. One of the photographs accompanying the story shows Soupy with Mayor Cobo presenting him with the proclamation.)

Unfortunately, the *New York Times* television critic was not amused by Soupy and his puppets' antics. Writing in his column on July 5, 1955, J. P. Shanley observed: "It was loud, unimaginative and annoying. It introduced hand puppets that behaved like seedy relations of those appearing on *Kukla, Fran and Ollie*...At times, Soupy himself suggested a combination of Pinky Lee and Jerry Lewis at their most obstreperous" (O'Connell 2008: 12-13). Such elitist criticism from the staid *Times* represented the kind of antagonism to the introduction to so-called children's shows of slapstick and zany comedy routines, owing much to Jewish-style humor, that Pinky Lee, Jerry Lewis, and Soupy Sales embodied.

Notwithstanding this criticism, Soupy and WXYZ would lobby the national office of ABC to pick up the *Lunch with Soupy Sales* show for national syndication. However, it would take over four years after the summer replacement before the Saturday noontime show would be aired nationally. On the other hand, after acquiring over one hundred "Betty Boop" cartoons in 1956, ABC would insist that the local station, Channel 7, incorporate them into its children programming (Boddy 1990: 169). This meant that "Betty Boop" cartoons would become a staple of Soupy's show before he aired on national television again. Those cartoons, while iconic in the 1930s, had so little appeal to Soupy's young audience that only one of my two dozen interviewees even mentioned it when questioned about which of the characters, cartoons, or routines on the lunchtime show were most memorable.

Nevertheless, more than a dozen of my interviewees recalled two other members of the puppet cast – Hippy the Hippo and Willie the Worm – and one young girl named "Peaches." When Soupy insisted that there be a rival puppet to Pookie, Hippy was created from a similar design that was, according to Jack Fleschig, "turned inside out." Willie the Worm was "a little latex accordion worm that was operated with a bulb in a tube." Because Willie was so delicate, he had to be constantly patched together. This may have been one of the reasons that Willie was known as "the sickest worm in Dee-troit." The live character of Peaches, who appeared toward the end of Soupy's time in Detroit, was actually Soupy in drag (Castelnero 2009: 18-19). Peaches, perhaps, indicated a nod to Milton Berle's appearances as a woman on his early 1950s show. In any case, all of these characters, whether puppets or live performers, delighted Soupy's young audience at lunchtime.

However, changes in programming at the local ABC affiliate, Channel 7, led to Soupy's lunchtime program being moved to an early breakfast show in October of 1958. Soupy's reflections on this move to the morning hour observe that "the networks saw that adults were actually watching TV at noontime, so they brought in performers like

Peter Lind Hayes and Liberace and put them on at noon and moved me to a morning time. It upset me because my audience was used to seeing me at noon and the whole concept of the shows, which was lunch with Soupy, didn't really make it at eight o'clock in the morning" (Sales 2001: 79). Actually, the breakfast show aired at 7:30 A.M., but did run for an hour. Up against what Soupy called "some mighty good competition from the networks in the form of NBC's *Today Show*," the show continued the basic format of the lunchtime show, just with more cartoons. Soupy would retain a strong fan base and the morning program, according to him, would "actually beat (the *Today Show*) in the ratings" (Sales 2001: 79).

Another afternoon show, called *Soupy's Ranch*, would have a short run on a Wednesday late afternoon time slot. As he recalls, "(the station) had no idea what they wanted the show to be, they just liked the name and figured I'd come up with some kind of concept" (Sales 2001: 79-80). That concept included showing old cowboy movies. Trying to juggle these different children's programs would eventually lead to a cancellation of Soupy's evening program and have an impact also on his personal life, something to be discussed in the next two chapters.

Although *Lunch with Soupy Sales* would continue on ABC on Saturday into 1961, the show no longer emanated from the WXYZ-TV studios. Soupy and some of the cast and crew moved to Los Angeles to air the syndicated program from the ABC affiliate there, KABC-TV. As Soupy recollects, "a few fellas thought I was nuts to leave." Soupy's own take on the move reflected his feeling that he "did everything I could do in Detroit" (Castelnero 2009: 29-30). Yet, what he did in Detroit on his daytime shows would become a template for much of what he was to do in Los Angeles and later in New York. On the other hand, the recognition that his audience was not confined to children meant that the craziness embedded in those daytime shows could be moved to an early evening slot as it would be in Los Angeles.

Since Soupy had operated in the late evening for most of his career on Detroit television, his time in the Motor City would not be complete without considering the evening program that also made him into the most popular television personality in Detroit in the 1950s. The next chapter will discuss that evening show, *Soupy's On*.

CHAPTER FIVE

SOUPY'S EVENING TV PROGRAM

In most respects, Soupy's evening show, *Soupy's On*, stood in stark contrast to *Lunch with Soupy Sales*. One could even say that the difference, literally and figuratively, seemed like night and day. At night Soupy was impeccably and conservatively dressed in a suit and tie unlike his noontime attire of big bow tie, floppy top hat, and black sweater. His lunchtime cast of characters consisted primarily of puppets whereas the evening program featured nationally prominent musicians and, after *Soupy's On* expanded to a half hour, a crew of live performers who enacted a variety of sketch comedy routines. Those manufactured sketches were scripted and rehearsed unlike the unscripted and loose format of *Lunch with Soupy Sales*. While children were the primary audience for the day programs, the evening show attracted mostly adults (except for those teens probably violating their curfew). Finally, at night Soupy did not have to contend with getting hit with pies and enduring other slapstick antics that befell him as the host of the noontime show.

When *Soupy's On* debut in September of 1953 at 11 P.M. on WXYZ-TV, it constituted a direct challenge to the news programming in that time slot. Initially, the show alternated between ten and fifteen minutes. After the three-year anniversary of *Soupy's On*, it changed to a half hour program, remaining that way in that time slot until three years later in 1959 when the show was cancelled. As with the daytime programs, very few episodes are known to exist. Hence, this chapter will rely on a variety of sources to reconstruct a semblance of what transpired on the show. Some of the content in this chapter will come from several interviews I conducted with those who had either direct or indirect connections with *Soupy's On* and a few of the original scripts found in various collections. Other substance will derive from cross-referencing the *Detroit Free Press* listing of guests on the show with a website called "The Concert Database," an incredible compilation of performances at Motor City venues that, in some cases, dates back to the 1930s. For the purposes of this chapter, the focus will be on those legendary jazz artists whose appearances at local clubs and venues during the 1950s allowed *Soupy's On* to feature them.

As Soupy made clear: "One of the great joys of the show was that I was able to invite many of the greatest jazz musicians and singers of the era, who often passed through Detroit as they toured the country in the mid-to-late 1950s" (Sales 2001: 74). For the most part, these jazz greats appeared as solo artists, backed up by the *Soupy's On* house band, a band under the direction of Hal Gordon, That band expanded from a quartet in the first few years to an octet in later years of the show. One of the consistent members of these different musical aggregations was Joe Messina, also one of my interviewees for this chapter. (Joe would achieve his own legendary status by becoming a key guitarist and arranger for Motown as part of what came to be known as the "Funk Brothers.") In addition to Joe's few stories about jazz artists, such as Charlie Parker, Miles Davis and Thelonious Monk who appeared on the show, the chapter will offer very brief biographical descriptions of highlighted performers. Supplementing these short bios, wherever possible, with those Motor City venues in which they could be seen at the time will give a further context for the jazz scene, already described at some length in Chapter Three.

Guitarist Joe Messina with house band for Soupy's On TV show

The first jazz performer that I found listed for *Soupy's On* was Earl "Fatha" Hines. According to the TV listings of the *Detroit Free Press*,

Hines was scheduled for a September 28, 1953 appearance on the evening program. (All further references to specific dates for these jazz musicians are drawn from the television pages of the archived *Free Press*.) He also had another listing for the first anniversary of the show on September 19, 1954. Hines was a legendary jazz pianist who came to prominence in the 1930s with an innovative "single-note line approach" to jazz piano (Jones 1967: 159). He was also a leader of a jazz orchestra in the 1940s that featured musicians, like Charlie Parker, who would form the vanguard for Bebop after leaving the band. During the 1940s Hines and his orchestra played the Paradise Theater, the premier venue on Woodward for Black musical entertainment. Formerly Orchestra Hall, it was taken over by Ben and Lou Cohen in 1941, running for over a decade and featuring other famous jazz bands, such as those headed by Count Basie and Duke Ellington. (Both would later be solo guests on *Soupy's On*.) When Hines made his appearance on Soupy's show, he was fronting a sextet at the Rouge Lounge.

Also showing up several times during the first year of *Soupy's On* was Johnny Hodges, the renowned alto sax player in Duke Ellington's orchestra. As one of the featured soloists with the Ellington ensemble, Hodges became well known for his distinctive glissando and vibrato sound. During the 1950s, Hodges headed up his own jazz combo. When Hodges turned up on Soupy's evening program on May 5, 1954, he was performing with his septet at the Crystal Show Bar. Because of Soupy's extensive knowledge of big band jazz and his obvious deference to the artistry of musicians like Johnny Hodges, the television audience to *Soupy's On* was not only treated to a showcase of legendary performers but also given a lesson on their role in establishing Black musicians, in particular, as pre-eminent American artists.

Another jazz legend whose gigs at the Crystal Show Bar in 1954 led to at least three different appearances on *Soupy's On* (April 7, July 16, and July 21) was Charlie Parker (Bjorn 2004: 114). Parker's incredible saxophone playing, especially on his electrifying alto work, set a standard that few, even now, can meet. His death in 1955 at the young age of thirty-four "turned Parker into an icon" (Kelley 2010: 185). Known as "Bird" to musicians and jazz fans alike, Parker's *Yardbird Suite* was, in fact, the theme song for *Soupy's On*. According to Joe Messina, when Parker requested to play his composition, *Groovin' High,* on the program, Hal Gordon had no familiarity at all with the tune. Since it was based on an old standard, *Whispering*, Joe gave the sheet music to that song, telling Gordon to just follow the chord structures. That performance by Parker and the house band apparently came off without a hitch. However, another time when Bird was scheduled to be at a rehearsal for Soupy's evening program, he was, according to Peter Stand, Executive Producer of *Soupy's On*, "very late. Actually, he didn't show up until the show was almost on," having stopped to see a movie. (Sales 2001: 77-78).

Strand recounts another mishap that involved the peerless jazz vocalist, Billie Holiday, when "she brought her little Chihuahua with her to rehearsal." Apparently trying to best White Fang as "the meanest dog in the world," Holiday's dog bit Strand. In order to make sure that the Chihuahua didn't have rabies, a doctor suggested keeping the dog under observation for two weeks. This, in turn, led to Billie Holiday putting her schedule on hold for that time period (Sales 2001: 77). While Strand did not provide a time frame for this incident, it's possible that that this coincided with Holiday's extended two-week appearance at the Rouge Lounge in October of 1954 or the three one-week performances at the Flame Show Bar in May of 1956 and 1957 or September of 1958. Less than a year after her last show at the Flame, Bill Holiday passed away at the young age of forty-five from a variety of afflictions.

The Flame Show Bar was one of the leading clubs in Detroit to spotlight jazz vocalists like Billie Holiday. In fact, two other well-known jazz singers, Chris Connor and Anita O'Day, played the Flame Show Bar around the same time that they made an appearance on Soupy's night program. Both O'Day and Connor were among the premier jazz singers in the 1950s, gaining popular and critical attention. Connor first attracted notice with Claude Thornhill's band in the 1940s. She also sang with Jerry Wald, one of Soupy's favorite orchestras, dating back to his time in high school in Huntington West Virginia. (Wald's big band played in Detroit in 1945 and 1946. According to the *Detroit Free Press*, Wald also was a guest soloist on April 25, 1957 for *Soupy's On*.) Connor showed up for an April 15, 1954 gig on *Soupy's On*. Three months later on July 23, Anita O'Day was the guest for Soupy's evening program. O'Day had been the vocalist with a number of jazz bands, including Gene Krupa's, Woody Herman's, and Stan Kenton's, before striking out on her own. During that time on her own, she experienced a bust or two for marijuana and later for heroin.

Two other jazz greats ravaged by drug problems during this period were trumpeters Chet Baker and Miles Davis. Baker's smooth style on trumpet, reflecting the West Coast jazz sound, carried over when he put down his horn and began to sing. His two-week stint at the Rouge Lounge in March of 1954 coincided with a March 8 appearance on *Soupy's On.* Davis's attempt to kick his heroin addiction during several months spent in Detroit was covered briefly in Chapter Three. As noted, Miles returned again and again to Detroit in the 1950s, playing all the major jazz clubs, like the Blue Bird Inn and Crystal Show Bar, in addition to numerous gigs at the Graystone Ballroom. According to several sources, Miles appeared at least half a dozen times on Soupy's evening show. While I haven't been able to pinpoint the exact dates, I do know that one of those times came during the period when the house band on *Soupy's On* included an accordion player. According to Joe Messina, that accordionist had never heard Miles before and his only comment after Davis's performance on the program was that he, Davis, needed a lesson!

No one who saw the young phenomenon, Clifford Brown, play a medley on his trumpet of *Lady Be Good* and *Memories of You* on *Soupy's On* would have the temerity to tell "Brownie" he required lessons. His brief, but stellar, jazz artistry was cut short when he died in a fatal car crash at the end of June 1956 at the age of twenty-six. Only weeks before he and his co-combo leader, the drummer Max Roach, had performed at the Rouge Lounge. They also played the Rouge at the beginning of 1956. That gig may have been around the time when he did the medley for Soupy's evening program. While that presentation is one of the few visual recordings of jazz acts still extant from *Soupy's On*, it is also the only known film footage of Clifford Brown. At the conclusion of Brownie's musical performance, Soupy does a brief, but respectful and knowledgeable, interview with the stellar trumpet player.

Another one of those available excerpts from the musical presentations on Soupy's evening show featured the brilliant and unique pianist, Erroll Garner. (Like Garner, my father was also born and raised in Pittsburgh. As a part-time bassist, my dad had the great fortune to sit in once with Garner for a brief number as a substitute bassist.) Garner's *Concert by the Sea* album had recently been released to popular and critical acclaim when he came to Detroit to play at Baker's Keyboard Lounge in January of 1956. His appearance on *Soupy's On* probably dates from early 1956, especially since Soupy is holding a copy of the *Concert by the Sea* album when introducing Garner. Praising Garner and that album, Soupy, once again, demonstrates his commitment to artists, like Garner, and the jazz they expertly perform. In turn, the obvious authenticity of Soupy's commentary reinforces his own venerable television personality.

While numerous jazz musicians, like Garner and others, performed on the evening program without designated dates, there are exact dates for when the tenor sax players, Coleman Hawkins and Lester Young, two other jazz legends, turn up on *Soupy's On*. For Coleman Hawkins, aka the "Hawk," his time on Soupy's evening show was March 29, 1954 during the period when he and his group were at the Crystal Show Bar. For Lester Young, aka "Prez," his moment on *Soupy's On* was June 23, 1954 while he also played the Crystal Show Bar. Both Hawkins and Young were members of jazz orchestras in the 1930s. They both developed distinctive styles that established them as the premier players of the tenor sax for modern jazz. As LeRoi Jones (aka Amiri Baraka) notes in his classic study of African American music, *Blues People*: "It was the growing prominence of the saxophone in the big band and the later elevation of that instrument to its fullest expressiveness by Coleman Hawkins that planted the seed for the kind of jazz played even today. However, it was not until the emergence of Lester Young that jazz became a saxophone or reed music" (Jones 1967: 158).

There were several other jazz musicians who were guests on *Soupy's On* during the first year of its telecast. The bassist, Slam Stewart, took time off from his gig with Art Tatum at Baker's Keyboard Lounge to do Soupy's evening show on November 17, 1953. Two legendary vibraphone players, Milt Jackson, born and bred in Detroit, and Terry Gibbs, a regular on Steve Allen's late 1950s evening program, the original *Tonight Show*, appeared for the *Soupy's On* television listing on February 1, 1954 and May 20, 1954, respectively. Jackson had returned to Detroit in between studio sessions for his new and soon-to-become famous combo, the Modern Jazz Quartet (Stryker 2019: 35-43). Gibbs had his own combo, starring at the Crystal Show Bar during May of 1954.

Jackson represented a number of jazz players from Detroit who gained national prominence and came back to do a solo gig on *Soupy's On*. Frank Rosolino, the outstanding trombonist in the Stan Kenton band, appeared on Soupy's show on May 11, 1954. Although Wardell Gray, tenor sax player, was not born in Detroit, as Rosolino was, he, nonetheless, attended Detroit's Cass Tech before heading off to join a number of swing big bands, including Count Basie's. He blew in as a guest on August 9, 1954. Other Detroit musicians who achieved distinction as jazz artists and were part of a roster of those who showed up for Soupy's evening program included the pianist, Tommy Flanagan, and the baritone sax player, Pepper Adams. (Bjorn 2004: 142-45. I saw and talked to Adams in the mid 1960s at the Crawford Grill, one of the premier jazz clubs in Pittsburgh).

Another great jazz reed player from Detroit, Yusef Lateef, is reputed to have been a guest on *Soupy's On (Detroitkidshow.com)*. Born as William Huddleston in Chattanooga in 1920, he came with his family to Detroit in 1925, the year before Soupy was born. Under the name of Bill Evans, Lateef worked with numerous big bands in the 1940s, including Dizzy Gillespie's Bebop orchestra. (The other Bill Evans was, of course, the superlative pianist for Miles Davis and part of his sextet that recorded the iconic *Kind of Blue* album in the late 1950s). When he returned to Detroit in the early 1950s, he sought out gigs at night. Because of his daytime job at the Chrysler Jefferson Ave plant, he had a difficult time of making it as a jazz musician. Eventually, however, he became a leader of his own aggregation in the mid-1950s, performing in 1957 and 1958 as a regular at Klein's Show Bar on 12th Street in Detroit (Bjorn 2004: 153-61; Stryker 2019: 26-34).

A number of other jazz legends can be found in a variety of photographs taken when they were with Soupy during his evening show although there is no precise date on any of those that I have seen. For example, there is a wonderful photograph of Soupy, stylishly attired in a sport coat and vest, standing next to Duke Ellington (Sales 2001: 73. It should be noted that one of my interviewees was so impressed by Soupy's fashion flair that he styled himself after Soupy and the jazz drummer, Art Blakey.). Since Duke Ellington and his Orchestra were the headliners at the Graystone Ballroom in 1954, 1956, and 1957, it's possible that Ellington showed up at the Channel 7 Studios in the Maccabees Building just a little north of where the Graystone was. The photo might also be dated from their joint presence on October 18, 1954 for a United Foundation event in Detroit. (This and many other public appearances by Soupy will be covered in the next chapter.)

Another undated photograph from *Soupy's On* is of the tenor sax standout, Illinois Jacquet, who appeared at various jazz venues in Detroit from 1954 to 1957. Any one of these times could have provided opportunities for him to appear as a guest for Soupy's show.

Given Soupy's commitment to showcasing jazz musicians on his evening show, it is not surprising that he was invited to be the master of ceremonies for a number of concerts in the Motor City during this period. Among one of the more intriguing of these emcee roles was that advertised for "Frank Brown's Battle of Jazz," featuring the bands of Stan Kenton and Count Basie, performing at the Graystone Ballroom on July 29, 1955. Soupy was not only listed as the MC, but also as the "Referee." It seems, however, when it came to financial rewards, Kenton and his large orchestra had already won this contest since his band was the first to gross a million dollars in one year and have a short-lived television program on CBS. (Of course, the disparity between what white and Black musicians were paid was not new and was reflective of the larger context of racial discrimination.) Another occasion for Soupy to act as the master of ceremonies was for what was billed as the "International Festival of Music" at Masonic Auditorium on February 16, 1957. The featured jazz performers included the Ted Heath band (a British big band probably on its first tour of the U.S.), Al Hibbler, the sightless African American singer who, after his eight year run as a vocalist with Duke Ellington, had a number of pop chart hits, including "Unchained Melody," June Christy, the cool jazz vocalist who started with Stan Kenton's band, and jazz pianist, Eddie Haywood, who had a hit single in 1956 with his composition, "Canadian Sunset." The latter three musicians probably all made solo guest appearances on Soupy's evening show.

In practically all those instances, these remarkable jazz musicians performed either by themselves or with the *Soupy's On* house band. One exception to this routine came about most likely in late September or early October of 1959 with the Thelonious Monk Quartet, then appearing at the Club 12 Show Bar, formerly Klein's Show Bar. For a number of reasons, Monk's performances at the club neither satisfied him nor the Detroit audience (Kelley 2010: 273-74). So, Monk may have been a little out of sorts when he brought his combo with him to the *Soupy's On* show. According to Joe Messina, the exceptional and idiosyncratic pianist and his quartet played his famous composition, "'Round Midnight," for a lengthy seventeen or eighteen minutes rather than the seven minutes allotted to them. The intensity and length of this mini-Monk concert led Soupy to sign off by referring to tomorrow's program as the Thelonious Monk show.

Had this been Monk's first television appearance, there might have been a reasonable explanation for his neglect of the time constraints on his quartet's performance other than his dogged determination to play the lengthy version of "'Round Midnight." In fact, several years earlier Steve Allen had welcomed Monk to his *Tonight Show* for Monk's debut on television. Monk joined a list of prominent jazz artists, like Earl Hines, Coleman Hawkins, Lester Young, Dizzy Gillespie, Duke Ellington, and Billie Holiday, who would grace the late night Steve Allen show. Of course, all of the aforementioned musicians, along with myriad others, had been or would be guests on *Soupy's On.* Given the national syndication of the *Tonight Show,* however, Steve Allen was recognized by the jazz critic, Leonard Feather, as "the greatest friend jazz had in television" (Kelley 2009: 187). While later acknowledging the incredible talent of the young Detroit jazz artists, Feather neglected to recognize the ground breaking and longer tenure of Soupy as a supporter and friend of jazz in television.

To counter the intensity of presentations by jazz artists like Monk, and to fill up the half hour allotted to *Soupy's On*, Soupy and his live crew put on comedic sketches. In many respects, these were "put ons" or parodies, similar to what Sid Caesar enacted on his shows. Soupy, along with director Pete Strand, wrote the scripts for these sketches, a few of which will be reviewed at the end of this chapter. Soupy's comedy cohorts would rehearse from these scripts, finishing with one last run-through at 10 P.M. (Golick 2009). According to Soupy, "We created a whole cast of zany, broad satirical characters, in the irreverent tradition of Sid Caesar and Ernie Kovacs, to whom I've sometimes been compared" (Sales 2001: 74). With a nod to the comic inventions of Caesar and Kovacs, Soupy and his crew manufactured skits for his evening program without the budget or national exposure and syndication of the aforementioned comedians. Nevertheless, Soupy brought to WXYZ-TV a daring version of satirical skits that enhanced his television personality.

What follows below is Soupy's recounting of these characters he crafted and acted out on *Soupy's On*, starting in 1957 until 1959:

> Charles Vichyssoise – kind of a composite of Charles Boyer, Maurice Chevalier, and Charles Aznavour – a leering, oily, "continental crooner" who was constantly arguing with the pianist and trading insults with surly patrons at the Club ChiChi. With a quick change I'd transform myself into Wyatt Burp, a seedy, power-belching sheriff, or the Lone Stranger (or, at other times, the Lone Rider), a...cowboy hero. Then there was Calypso King Harry Bella, who was actually nothing at all like Belafonte, but a wild-eyed South American with a Moe Howard hairdo who made his living rolling drunks. We also had a spot called "Author Meets Critic," wherein I played host Ernest Hemingbone (maybe actually Herringbone), a pipe-smoking writer who sniped at his literary rivals. I think, all in all, we must have created thirty or so different characters (Sales 2001: 74).

Of course, there were other actors who performed in these comedy sketches, becoming, in effect, co-conspirators with Soupy in the satirical zaniness that prevailed on the evening show, and, in the case of a few, television personalities in their own right, albeit lesser-known, not as well-paid, and lacking in the larger adulation that Soupy attained. Among the best known and loved of these actors was Rube Weiss. Prior to becoming a cast member for *Soupy's On*, Weiss had been on WXYZ radio programs, such as *The Lone Ranger* and the *Green Hornet.* Outside of his career in radio and television as an actor and director, Weiss taught drama classes for a time during the early 1950s at Northern High School in Detroit. In his capacity as director for WXYZ-TV, Weiss gained the admiration of his colleagues, one of whom claimed, "he had a heart of gold" (Kiska 2005: 212-13).

According to Rube Weiss's son, Leon, one of the roles his Dad played on Soupy's evening show, that of "Shoutin' Shorty Hogan," was, far and away, the most memorable supporting character. Shoutin' Shorty Hogan was "a lovable but weird songwriter and piano player. My Dad would sit at the piano and play for Soupy and the assembled his latest 'hit.' They shot those bits without showing my Dad's hands as the bandleader, Hal Gordon, would supply the keyboard tomes off camera. The songs were silly and irreverent. One that I recall was 'I gave my baby red roses, and she gave me halitosis!'" Leon also recalls that his Dad would be recognized all over Metro Detroit with folks hollering: "Hey, it's Shoutin' Shorty Hogan from the Soupy show. Hey Shorty, loved this week's song!" Rube would then often respond by "singing a few bars of the latest silly ditty."

Another member of the evening cast was actually better known than Rube Weiss since he was a regular on Soupy's noontime program. Of course, Clyde Adler never showed his face on Soupy's daytime show. As White Fang and Black Tooth on *Lunch with Soupy Sales*, Clyde's presence was off-camera, manipulating large furry paws and making crazy sounds. Although Clyde did not hide behind on-stage puppets for *Soupy's On*, he, nonetheless, appeared in a variety of costumes that conformed to the range of characters he played. A few of those acting roles were "Kudda-dux, a turbaned Indian," "Jefferson, a Mississippi gambler" and "Waco in the Wyatt Burp cowboy takeoff" (Boyd, *Detroit Free Press*, 11/17/1957: TV 14). It was as Waco that Clyde experienced one of those inevitable mishaps that plagued live TV. His fake beard fell off.

Another accident happened to one of the other members of the sketch comedy cast of *Soupy's On*. Bertha Forman, "a veteran of 50 years on stage, radio, and television," was supposed to remain seated while the guest vocalist sang a tune called "Timber." Instead, she fell off the bench where she sat, startling the singer. Soupy had to intervene and finish the song. Bertha managed to avoid any other mishaps even as she played a range of characters from "Drunken Sadie" to "Baby Doll." Commenting on that latter role, Forman told Robert Boyd of the Detroit *Free Press*: "Imagine me wearing a man's night shirt and sucking my thumb in that silly crib!" Her most popular role as Soupy's "Mother-in-Law, in which she trades pleasantries with him while her 'inner voice' tears him apart in previously taped asides," led to her being introduced "everywhere...as Soupy's Mother-in-Law" (11/17/1957: TV 14).

A much younger female cast member, Jane Hamilton, never had to contend with being mistaken for Soupy's Mother-in-Law. The characters she portrayed were much younger and stereotypically blonde birdbrains, identified, for example as a "ditzy literary critic Harriet Van Loon and the hip-swinging floozy, Bubbles." Performing Harriet during the last month of her pregnancy, Jane had to laugh hysterically in that role. Soupy broke character to inquire whether she was going to give birth right then and there. Another time Jane had a chance to respond in character with a nasty zinger of a gag. With Soupy acting as a defense attorney, Jane's character confessed to shooting "her husband with a bow and arrow so's not to wake the kiddies" (Boyd, *Detroit Free Press*, 11/17/1957: TV 14).

The final member of the *Soupy's On* cast discussed by Robert Boyd in his *Free Press* article was Leon McNew. Appearing on other WXYZ television shows, McNew would show up every now and then to take on "the role of Mike Walters, relentless interviewer" (maybe a satirical poke at Mike Wallace who then was doing evening television interview shows, including one for the ABC network in 1957.) As Mike Walters, McNew would grill Soupy playing the "teenage idol Elvis Pretzel or calypso-singer Harry Bella" (11/17/1957: TV 14).

While the cast for the sketch comedy routines would rotate, depending on the scripted roles, certain characters were built into longer running bits, like the "Lone Rider," sometimes referred to as the "Lone Stranger." In a 1958 script for the "Lone Rider," previously unpublished and hidden amidst some old notebooks of Soupy's now in the possession of Kathy O'Connell, the parody of the *Lone Ranger* television show is very evident. Soupy, of course, plays the masked stranger and Rube Weiss is his faithful Indian companion, "Pronto." The sketch is introduced by the kind of voice-over that begins the TV series; only the *Soupy's On* version satirizes the pious clichés that accompany the intro to the *Lone Ranger*. As written in the script, the Voice calls out: "From the old west come the thundering hooves and the man who tamed the plains...men, women, and children loved him...but others hated his guts! It's the Lone Rider and his raunchy (sic!) friend Pronto...Hi Ho Sterling (instead of Silver) awayyy!"

Leon McNew, Jane Hamilton, Clyde Adler, Bertha Forman and Soupy

Soupy and Cast of the Comedy Skits on Soupy's On television program

The setting for the "Lone Rider" is a saloon. Pronto enters first, requesting a drink from the bartender who refuses to serve him because he is an Indian. Pronto's response is to say it's all a disguise and dons a Jimmy Durante nose to prove it. Then, the Lone Rider enters the bar in a crouching position ("Just in case he is shot, he doesn't have far to fall.") The Lone Rider will face off with the corrupt Sheriff who is unavailable between the hours of 10 and 3 because he's robbing banks. Trying to screw up his courage, the Lone Rider claims he is "gonna clean up this town and fight any man who doesn't abide by the law." Challenged by the rather large Sheriff, probably played by the 6 foot 4, 350 pound WXYZ-TV telecine operator, Jim Powers, the Lone Rider decides the better part of valor is to "beat it" out of town. When the Sheriff calls the Lone Rider a "chicken," Pronto intervenes, forcing the Lone Rider to reconsider. In the meantime, there's a cackle and an egg materializes next to the Lone Rider. The Sheriff then threatens Pronto by calling on his "hired gun" – the "Ringo Kid"-whose falsetto voice is reminiscent of the Sid Caesar sketch about the silent movie star who can't make the transition to the talkies because of his high-pitched voice. In any case, the Lone Rider sketch dissolves into a chaotic fight without a resolution of the triumph of good over evil that was a hallmark of *The Lone Ranger* television series as well as other westerns of the time.

Lone Stranger Detroit Free Press Ad

A parody of the 1950s weekly TV series, *Person to Person*, featuring the well-known and respected reporter and interviewer, Edward R. Murrow, allows Soupy and his cast another opportunity to satirize film and television programs and celebrity stars. As Ted Burrow, Soupy becomes the intrepid interviewer of various movie idols on the comedy sketch called "Folk to Folk." In one of the scripts dated 1958, "Folk to Folk," aka "Meet the Stars," Burrow shows up at the Beverly Hills home of Johnny Wisenheimer, an obvious send-up of Johnny Weissmuller, world class swimmer in the 1920s, star of the Tarzan films of the 1930s and 1940s and Jungle Jim movie and television series of the 1950s. After having been fired from his last picture that the producer alleged was more "panned than the popcorn," Johnny is trying to resurrect his fading career. Having a starlet share screen time with him in his new film, *Tarzan Swings Again*, Johnny is hoping that the added romance will attract an audience.

While the sketch comedy routines relied on parodies of real or imaginary personalities, some of the other skits performed on *Soupy's On* turned on single gags and short jokey bits. For example, in one of the scripts posted on the *Detroitkidshow* website, one can find the following exchanges between "Manny Street," the straight man in the "man-on-the-street program" that "let's you meet the man on the street." When Manny asks "What is your occupation," the man on the street responds, "I used to be an elevator operator, but they fired me." "What happened?" "Nothing happened – I just couldn't remember the route!" Another man on the street answers to what he does for a living: "I'm a plumber." Manny Street inquires, "May I ask why you became a plumber?" "My girl always said she...likes a man with a pipe." The plumber also mentions his "sideline" as a "magician who saws a woman in half." In response to whether he's any good, the plumber and part-time magician answers: "I got two half sisters to prove it!"

Not all of the comedy on *Soupy's On* was in front of the camera. Several incidents involving the telecasting of live commercials on the evening show created their own strange, and sometimes humorous, moments. One of the most recounted of these advertising snafus involved a man with a wooden leg rescuing Soupy from a potentially aborted beer commercial. The confirmation that this was a real and not made-up or staged event can be found in Dick Osgood's Column on April 25, 1957 on the TV page of the *Detroit Free Press* and verified by my interview with Joe Messina. In any case, Soupy's account of this event deserves to be quoted in full:

> On this particular night, it came time to do a beer commercial. At the end of the commercial, I was supposed to be pouring a beer lifting it and saying, "Altas Beer (more correctly spelled as "Altes," a local brew that later became an official sponsor of the Detroit Tigers and Detroit Lions), to your health...So, I'm just about ready to do that and the stage manager says, "Where's the beer opener?" And one of the stagehands, looking aghast, says, "I don't have an opener. I left it downstairs." (Shooting live from either the 14th or 15th floor of the Maccabees Building meant there wasn't enough time to retrieve a can opener from the main floor below.) Well, if we weren't able to do the commercial as it was written, we would

have to make good on it, which meant losing money by giving them a free commercial, so as you can imagine there was a little panic. Suddenly, a guy in a checkered jacket, with gray hair and a goatee, wearing an ascot and standing to the side, said, "Do you want me to open it for you?" So, I reach out to hand him the bottle and as he comes towards me I see that he's walking a little funny. He takes the bottle, puts his foot on the table and I see that he has a wooden leg. On the inside of the wooden leg, he has a bottle opener. He opens the bottle, and that's the last thing that was said on the show. I fell down on the floor laughing. We never did find out who he was, but it was just about the wildest thing I ever saw (Sales 2001: 75).

Another occurrence with a flawed commercial presentation had the crew in stitches at Soupy's expense. As related by Peter Strand, the Executive Producer and Co-writer of *Soupy's On*: "Because we were a live TV show, there were many times when things didn't go exactly as planned. We were at the Maccabees Building (where we had) a few long-term sponsors, one of which was a local car dealer. We would have cars in the studios, different cars on different nights – with Soupy doing the commercials. I remember, he had a hand mike which would only go so far – actually, we thought it would go a little farther than it did – and one night he almost strangled himself with it. But he just continued doing the commercial. He went with the flow. We were laughing and crying at the same time, watching him. But nothing really fazed Soupy" (Sales 2001: 77).

There were also other commercials not done by Soupy that caused something of a commotion on the live set. One of those commercials concerned the Restocraft Mattress Company with its curvaceous spokeswomen, Loree Marks. As "the White Camellia," Marks was a host for daytime movies on WXYZ-TV. In the evening, she would slip into something more comfortable and promote Restocraft mattresses. The director of this nighttime ad related what happened during one of these commercial spots featuring Marks: "One night while they were doing a mattress commercial and Loree was reclining on the mattress in a low cut, sexy negligee, her push up bra lost it's control and suddenly, there was more of Loree exposed than there should have been. They immediately cut to Soupy on the other side of the studio and he totally lost it. I don't think much happened for the next couple of minutes except for a lot of laughing and embarrassment all around" (Golick, *Soupy's On, Detroitkidshow.com*).

While Soupy, the cast, and crew for *Soupy's On* worked their way through these live televised mishaps, often joining the viewing audience in surprised laughter, there was also a small in-studio audience that got caught up in the accidental frivolity. When Rube Weiss brought his two sons to the WXYZ-TV studio to see him on set, there was a minor mishap involving Leon and a Big Boy burger. Recalling what transpired, Leon wrote to me as follows: "Big Boy restaurants was one of the sponsors and the owners, the Elias brothers, would have a large order of Big Boy burgers and fries delivered to the studio for live commercials and to be eaten by the crews. My dad made sure Dave and I got our Big Boy burgers and I remember one time I let out a big belch when Soupy's guest star Buddy Greco was singing, causing a burly stage hand to give me a firm reprimand." Whether the burp got picked up during the live performance by Buddy Greco will never be known since the kinoscope of this show, like most of the others, was destroyed. Maybe it would have more easily blended into "Wyatt Burp," the parody that Soupy and Rube did on numerous occasions for the evening show.

It is very clear that *Soupy's On* had a vocal and loyal following, encouraged to watch by the ads placed in the TV section of the Detroit *Free Press* in 1957 and 1958. Those ads, in particular, highlighted the different characters and sketches that Soupy would enact during his nighttime program. When Soupy took time off for a vacation, the audience response, reflected in the letter to the *Free Press* below, gives some indication of how popular and highly regarded Soupy was. The full letter, signed by the Hartz family, appeared in the July 14, 1957 edition of the *Free Press* on page 67 and reads as follows: "Although TV performers do need vacations, and rightfully deserve them, we feel the replacement should, at least, be in keeping with the high standard set by the regular performer. A case in point is that of Soupy Sales 11 P.M. program. WXYZ-TV seems to employ many capable persons who could do a fine job of substituting should the occasion arise. Mickey Shorr (no relation) is not one of these persons. Mr. Shorr's handling of Soupy's show is not in the best of taste and his presentation of commercials would dissuade any viewer from purchasing the product. The talent seen since Soupy has gone has been very poor also. This is one family who will switch to the News at 11 P.M. until Soupy comes back to give us the entertainment we enjoyed so much before he left."

The recognition of Soupy's talent in this aforementioned letter is not only a testament to him and the evening show, but also reflects the strong allegiance of his viewers to both. Soupy and Channel 7 nurtured that devotion through countless personal appearances during his time in the Motor City, promoting him as a premier television personality. The next chapter will consider the wide variety of Soupy's personal appearances and how he built a loyal following for his emergence as the most popular local television personality in Detroit during the 1950s.

Chapter Six

Public Persona and Private Life

Crafting a public persona that generated a large and loyal following, Soupy Sales sought to complement the audience that watched his daytime and evening programs. His life outside the WXYZ-TV studios entailed engaging and entertaining his thousands of fans in Metro Detroit. The promotion and publicity that inhered in manufacturing his television personality accompanied his public persona (Bennett 2011: 18). Peter Strand remembers what often transpired when Soupy would show up for a last minute appearance around town: "Soupy did a lot of guest appearances and I would go with him. We would go to a Big Boy restaurant, one of our sponsors, and the crowd would be enormous. Soupy might just announce it casually on his show, 'Hey, I'm going to be dropping by Big Boy…tomorrow afternoon,' and thousands of people would show up to see him. And he'd stand there and sign autographs for a good hour. Other than a newsperson, it's rare for a personality to last on local television, especially for variety performers, but Soupy sure did. He was Mr. Detroit, for so many years" (Sales 2001: 79).

Soupy's desire to be out in public derived from his own personal inclinations and the economic imperatives of television stations and their sponsors. Acknowledging that he was a "workaholic" who "loved (show) business," he also believed that he "owed it to the people of Detroit" to do personal appearances for which he was not financially compensated (Sales 2001: 84). According to Dave Usher, Soupy's personal manager for part of his time in Detroit, "he would average about five or six calls a day from viewers asking, mainly because of his kids show, if he'd make appearances at various locations. So, we'd show up wherever and Soupy would dress up in the garb he wore on the show, the high hat and his oversized polka-dot-red-and-white bow tie and in a sweater and a shirt – that was his costume" (Sales 2001: 70-1). In fact, it was the children's show that spun off the formal organization of the Birdbath Club with memberships and events, especially at local movie theatres. Kids could "send a dime or something" to United Dairies, one of the sponsors for *Lunch with Soupy Sales*, and get in return "a membership card...and a little button" (Castelnero 2009: 27). Those Birdbath events (to be discussed in more detail later in this chapter) drew thousands of fans. Soupy asserts that he was "really appreciative of the fans because I had never done a show like that before...and doing the show I could tell it was catching on, and I never forgot that with the people" (Castelnero 2009: 29).

It's also clear from the archives of the Detroit *Jewish News* that Soupy did not want to forget his own connections to the Jewish community. Starting in the fall of 1953 right through the fall of 1959, he participated in a variety of events as a master of ceremonies or special guest. One of those guest appearances, announced well in advance in the Detroit *Jewish News* on October 16, 1953, was providing the entertainment for a Hanukah party sponsored by several of the local Jewish War Veterans posts. Another event, supported by Jewish War Vets, that featured Soupy was a fundraiser for Children's Hospital in the summer of 1954. That fall he appeared at a children's party sponsored by Temple Israel's Men's Club. Soupy also worked with a number of PTA's at schools where Jewish kids predominated. Even when he and his family were no longer living in the Jewish neighborhoods of Northwest Detroit, Soupy would be invited to participate in a Jewish-backed event. For example, he and Rube Weiss from the *Soupy's On* show were the speakers at an October 1959 panel on "What Makes it Funny" at the Jewish Community Center in Northwest Detroit.

Another fascinating aspect of Soupy's connections to the Jewish community was the number of "sightings" of Soupy in those Northwest Detroit neighborhoods during the mid 1950s. Among my Jewish interviewees, stories about these sightings abounded. Barry Hoffman maintains that when he and his family would eat dinner at Darby's, an upscale Jewish deli on 7 mile near Wyoming in Northwest Detroit, he would see Soupy greeting people as they came in through the door. Any number of other interviewees claimed that Soupy lived just a few blocks away from their homes in the Jewish neighborhoods. One person insisted that he saw Soupy drive by in a limousine. It seems that Soupy sightings attained a kind of apocryphal status almost equaling those of Elvis. The difference, of course, was that those Elvis sightings occurred after he passed away; whereas, for Soupy, it was wherever and whenever he passed by during his heyday in the Motor City.

When Soupy and his family moved to Grosse Pointe in 1958, the sightings persisted, supplemented, however, by actual contacts between other residents of that tony suburb and the Sales family. Frank Joyce, who grew up in the middle class suburb of Royal Oak, thought he saw Soupy at a football game between his high school, Royal Oak Dondero, and Grosse Pointe High. As he remembered in his interview with me, he experienced "teen disillusionment" because Soupy, as a Grosse Pointer, had probably become "a snobby rich person." In contrast to Frank's perception of Soupy's snobbishness, one of the younger neighbors of Soupy and his family had a contrasting real encounter. Crispin Cioe, a twelve-year old living nearby (later to become a highly regarded musician and record producer), approached Soupy's house after a snowstorm to "ask if he needed his walk shoveled. He said yes, paid me fairly, and this led to my clearing his sidewalk a couple more times that winter...I remember feeling that shoveling that sidewalk only strengthened my spiritual rapport and ability to more fully savor the jokes on Soupy's show" (Sales 2001: 80 and 82).

A number of other encounters with Soupy by his young fans cemented that strong bond they and others felt with him and his daytime programs. Because Mike Harrison's Dad sold television advertising, he was fortunate enough to see a number of the live shows at the WXYZ-TV studio in the Maccabees Building. Peggy Tibbits, whose father played "Milky the Clown," met Soupy when he and her father appeared together on another show. Sitting next to Soupy, Peggy recalls, "I just remember being thrilled" (Castelnero 2009: 28). Accompanying his grandmother to her doctor's appointment in the Maccabees Building, Larry Dlusky ran into Soupy while waiting for the elevator. "He walked over to talk to me...I think I probably did all the talking. I told Soupy I was a member of the Birdbath Club and I had the magic slate that wrote in three colors...he seemed genuinely interested in what I was saying and was talking to me like an equal. That stayed with me the rest of my life – that he took the time to do that" (Castelnero 2009: 28-9). These qualities of ordinariness and authenticity, so central to the manufacturing of a television personality (Bennett 2011: 26-32), were also integral to Soupy's public persona.

It wasn't only chance encounters that reinforced the loyalty and respect that Soupy's young fans exhibited. As mentioned previously, the Birdbath Club provided an organized vehicle for Soupy's followers to join and show their support when he made public appearances under its auspices. As Soupy recollects, "it was another one of those gimmicks that worked out really wonderful" (Castelnero 2009: 26). Not only did it work out wonderfully for the kids, but also Soupy's reputation and celebrity status in Detroit expanded almost exponentially, as revealed in one of the more massive turnouts for a Birdbath Club event. As reported in the *Detroit Free Press* in the December 18, 1956 edition: "Soupy Sales was stuttering all day Monday. He couldn't get over the mob that showed up at the State Fair Coliseum on Sunday (December 16) for his Birdbath Party. Police estimated that there were 12,000 on hand" (33).

From 1956 through 1960, the *Free Press* carried countless advertisements for Soupy's personal appearance at the major downtown movie theatres for a Birdbath Club showing of cartoons, the Three Stooges, or Abbott and Costello films. Commenting on Soupy's frenetic schedule, the May 10, 1957 *Free Press* opined: "Soupy Sales is going to need a fast bicycle Saturday. He will be speeding between the Michigan, Palms, and Broadway Capitol Theatres for three meetings of his Birdbath Club" (23). Remembering the times that Soupy had his Birdbath events at the downtown Fox Theatre, Ed Golick reminisced: "He'd have these little things at the Fox Theatre, showing cartoons and joke around...and he would just fill up the Fox Theatre. People would be standing outside, wanting to get in" (Castelnero 2009: 27).

There were times, however, when Soupy's busy schedule wrought havoc for his adoring audiences, especially when the venue was too small to accommodate all of them. When Soupy turned up late for a "Fun Night" event at a Detroit elementary school for which he was the advertised guest, there was, according to a one of the organizers of the "Fun Night," "a junior-size riot." Although Soupy was only a half hour late and willing to do additional shows in order to accommodate everyone, some of the attendees were either angry or disconsolate. The woman who chaired the entertainment committee told the *Free Press:* "The parents caused more trouble than the children" (5/18/ 1954: 33. This is the same issue of the Detroit newspaper that featured on the front page the historic Supreme Court 9-0 decision on Brown v. Board of Education.). Fortunately, things quieted down without having to call the police to quell the disturbance.

Mid 1950s Marque from downtown Detroit Fox Theatre

On the other hand, Dave Usher remarked on the need for police intervention at times when Soupy appeared in public. "Many times when we'd go for personal appearances, we'd really need a police escort. It's had to believe, but Soupy was more recognizable than President Eisenhower. He...had this kind of recognition with adults, because of his evening show at eleven o'clock which would usually beat out his competition." Even when Soupy showed up unannounced in public, crowds would gather once it was known that Soupy was present. Dave Usher recollects another time when Soupy accompanied him to the County Courthouse that "we heard a roar. We looked around and saw that it was coming from a crowd of people. They were chanting, 'Soupy, Soupy, Soupy.' Evidently, word had gotten out that he was going to be at the courthouse. I remember we walked around toward the parking lot, and looking up at the buildings around us we could see people standing in the windows...yelling 'Hi, Soupy.' That's how popular he was" (Sales 2001: 70 and 72).

Soupy's popularity, and even adulation, as reflected in the incidents cited above, can be attributed, to a great extent, to the kind of visual recognition facilitated by his television shows. That recognition, reinforced by the intimacy Soupy enacted on his daytime and evening shows, generated the celebrity status he acquired and the accompanying fan following. In his classic study of the impact of media culture on its consumers, Daniel Boorstin defined the celebrity as "a person who is well-known for their well-knownness" (Boorstin 1961: 58). (As Graeme Turner points out 2004: 4-5, Boorstin's perspective on celebrity was developed in the context of a somewhat elitist fear of the cultural change television was enabling.) Although Boorstin's definition is seemingly tautological, his perspective actually helps to reveal the psychological impact of visual recognition and its relationship to celebrity status (DeBacker 2012). In other words, Soupy's fans were reacting not only to Soupy as an "average guy" who happened to be a television personality, but also to how that television personality reached into the lives of his audience, enabling, in the process, "a positive, personal, (and) relatively deep emotional connection" (Duffet 2013: 2).

Soupy and WXYZ-TV engaged in a number of practices and promotions that facilitated connecting with his audience. One of the more unusual promotions involved the announcement in the *Detroit Free Press* in December 14, 1954 of a contest whose winner would have "Soupy and the Gang" (those from the *Soupy's On* show) entertain that person at a party at his/her residence. Sure enough, Soupy, along with his WXYZ-TV producer Pete Strand, and several members of the Hal Gordon band, including Gordon, bassist Harry Walker, clarinetist Clarence Hewitt, and guitarist, Joe Messina, showed up at Mrs. Joseph Cox's house in Detroit on January 14, 1955. As reported later in the *Free Press*, Mrs. Cox's winning entry in the contest "told of the party she wanted to give to celebrate her husband's admittance to the Michigan Bar Association after four years of combining night school and a daytime job" (1/23/1955: n.p.). According to the article and the associated photographs, the whole neighborhood was invited and Soupy entertained young and old alike.

During that same month, January, in 1955, Soupy helped to kickoff the March of Dimes fundraising drive at Grand Circus Park, one of the oldest downtown outdoor sites for large gatherings. This was one of many such public appearances in Detroit where Soupy's celebrity status brought his fans together with other interested folks. There were several instances where Soupy was part of the United Foundation

Torch Drive, usually conducted in October for volunteers. At least from 1954-1956, Soupy participated in the rather large entertainment extravaganza that signaled the start of the Torch Drive. The October 16, 1956 front page *Free Press* report on the previous Monday night's kickoff at the Broadway Capitol Theatre in downtown Detroit listed the following entertainers (a number of whom appeared around the same time on the *Soupy's On* show): Danny Kaye, Pee Wee Hunt, the Barry Sisters, Mel Torme, the Harmonicats, and Soupy Sales.

Soupy also was featured in a number of Easter and Christmas public celebrations for which his Jewish grandparents may have been spinning in their graves. Nonetheless, Soupy's catholic (meaning universal) approach to his personal appearances encompassed being a public part of these Christian holidays. An announcement in the *Detroit Free Press* on March 20, 1955 of an upcoming Variety Club sponsored Easter luncheon party at the Veterans Memorial Building spotlighted Soupy as one of the main entertainers (15). As far as Soupy's involvement with Christmas events, one manifestation of that was Muirhead's Giant Christmas Parade, advertised in the Comics section of the *Free Press* with the invitation to join with Soupy Sales, "Your Favorite TV star" (11/3/1955: 44). A few years later, Soupy was involved as an emcee for the Christmas Tree Lighting Ceremony on Woodward and Jefferson, the main intersection in downtown Detroit by the riverfront. The news item also listed Fran Allison, from *Kukla, Fran and Ollie*, who would be reading from *The Christmas Story* (*Free Press* 12/18/1957: 41). Soupy's participation in these Christmas and Easter events suggests a sensitivity to and understanding of the meaning and significance of such rituals to the majority non-Jewish audience.

In addition to these large public religious and secular gatherings, there were two special events in the mid 1950s of which Soupy was an integral part that tapped into the national popular and political culture of the period. The first took place over several days in mid June 1955 in the midst of the Davy Crockett craze. The second event was a "Greater Detroit Youth Rally" sponsored by the *Free Press* and Detroit High School Student Councils at Olympia Stadium on April 22, 1956, produced by Pete Strand and featuring Soupy, along with the Platters, other entertainers and politicians, like the popular Democratic Governor of Michigan, G. Mennen "Soapy" Williams, who was in the fourth of his six two-year terms. Before turning to the Soupy to Soapy rally, intended as countering the hysteria around "juvenile delinquency" in this era, Detroit's contribution to the Davy Crockett craziness will be highlighted, especially as a contrast to how Soupy's "typicality" and "familiarity" as a television personality (Bennett 2011: 7) are measured against the construction of a mythic figure like Davy Crockett and the national "mania" created around the Disney manufactured construction of that legendary character.

Davy Crockett "mania" emerged with the telecast in late 1954 and early 1955 of a special *Disneyland* series about Crockett's later life and death at the Alamo. (ABC and Disney thought it best not to show Crockett's actual death at the Alamo for the conclusion of the series.) The Crockett serial "garnered the highest ratings of the decade (and produced) a bonanza of product spinoffs" (Marling 1994: 124). Among the product spinoffs were the immensely popular coonskin caps which, according to cultural historian Steven Watts, became an "almost religious icon for American children in 1955 and 1956" (Watts 1997: 315). At the height of the Crocket craze these caps were selling around the country at the rate of 5,000 a day. In Detroit, the *Free Press* announced on the second front page of the June 12, 1955 edition that free caps printed by the newspaper would be available at J. L. Hudson's downtown department store and at all Hudson and Nash car dealers. Included in the same June 12 account was a notice of the next day appearance of the actor of Davy Crockett fame, Fess Parker, in front of massively large Hudson's store on Woodward in downtown Detroit.

Parker was traveling around the United States on a promotional tour for the new Disney movie, *Davy Crockett: King of the Wild Frontier*. In addition to his live appearance on June 13, Parker would be the guest on Soupy's noontime show on June 14. That day, the *Free Press*, under the large headline, "10,000 Little 'Davy Crocketts' Welcome Their Idol to Detroit," reported on the enormous crowd entertained by Parker and his co-star, Buddy Ebsen. The reporter, Louis Cook, touted the new folk hero while extolling the history lesson that Parker brought to life in his portrayal of Crockett (3). It seemed entirely appropriate that Cook also referred to the Crockett comic strip that would be starting in the *Free Press* on June 26 since Cook and Disney's sense of history was little more than the Cold War comic version of the real Davy Crockett (Marling 1994: 124; and Watts 1997: 317-19). This rendering of Crockett and the "aw-shucks" quality of Parker reinforced how such television stardom, in contrast to television personalities like Soupy, was built upon both national commercial publicity and the dominant ideology of the times.

If not one of the explicit purposes for the "Greater Detroit Youth Rally," the connection between the fear of juvenile delinquency and politically wayward youth was implicit in the call for and follow-up to the rally. In its announcement of the rally, the *Detroit Free Press* editorialized, "the program will serve to recognize the majority of Greater Detroit youth are making contributions to the community" (4/19/1956: 3). The follow-up front-page *Free Press* article, under the headline of "16,000 Youths Pledge a Better Future," (4/23/1956), reported on how every one of the invited speakers, from Governor "Soapy" Williams to Soupy Sales, stood up to cheer these young people. An adjacent column by Sydney Harris praised these youth who were contrasted with the "delinquent society" and those media that were viewed as contributing factors to juvenile delinquency (4/23/1956: 1). The panic about juvenile delinquency, so evident as the subtext of this event, was part of a larger dread related to the Cold War. As Ann Marie Kordas stresses in her book on *The Politics of Childhood in Cold War America*, "new worries about adolescents in the Cold War period may have encouraged adults to be more aware of what teenagers did…the reclassification of certain acts as underage drinking and sexual intercourse among adolescents as criminal offenses instead of moral issues best dealt with by parents or clergy may also have accounted for the increase in 'delinquency'" (Kordas 2014: 135).

Although Soupy's two sons, Tony and Hunt, were not teenagers during his time in Detroit, they did become part of the portrayal of the public persona of Soupy Sales. In an article by Myra MacPherson in the August 11, 1957 edition of the *Free Press* under the headline of "Soupy Tells Why Kids Love Him," there is an accompanying photograph of Soupy, Hunt (age 3), Tony (age 6) and his wife Barbara. The story connects their family life to his Detroit youthful fans and to future possibilities as a way to explain his popularity as a television personality. The opening paragraphs convey those connections: "Soupy Sales barely slurped the last glass of milk on his TV kiddie luncheon show before his followers descended. Walking out of the WXYZ-TV studio afterwards, the Detroit comic was trailed like the Pied Piper. Two pig-tailed girls who barely reached 6-foot Soupy's knees, held out slightly crumpled pictures for autographs. Two phones rang for him in the lobby and a teenage boy (not a delinquent for sure) asked, 'how's chances of a job.' Soupy spun around and in seconds had signed the pictures, made polite small talk on the phone, told the job seeker who to see" (TV-11).

Sprinkled throughout the rest of the story are Soupy's insights on his relationship with his audience, his own children, the future, and what he does to relax, all components of the links between his public persona and private life. On his bond with his older audience, Soupy observes in the same article: "Some performers are just noticed by people – but I'm always greeted like a long lost friend." (In this reference, one again sees how that sense of familiarity enables the manufacturing of a television personality. Moreover, this familiarity factor also tempered the kind of celebrity status Soupy achieved, making him much less remote and exotic than many other celebrities.) As far as being a father, Soupy comments: "Having my own kids helps me as a children's entertainer. Some entertainers who don't understand them talk down to kids all the time." The article also probes when or even whether he plans to leave Detroit for a bigger network show. "Reflecting on Sid Caesar's losing his show," MacPherson writes, "Soupy thinks it was just an unfortunate time spot" while calling Caesar a "genius" who has "enough talent to start his own medium." Finally, Soupy points to one way that he relaxes on Sunday "is to play ball with my baseball team" (MacPherson 8/11/1957: TV-11).

The following year, 1958, after Soupy had signed for a sixth season on WXYZ-TV, becoming Detroit's highest paid television performer, baseball and his family once again became stories of interest in the *Free Press*. The same newspaper writer, Myra MacPherson, interviewed his wife, Barbara, with the two kids at one of the baseball games between television teams. Trying to placate Tony with some gum, Barbara sighs, "We come to most of the games, but hardly ever see them. The kids come to eat popcorn, swing on the swings...But Soupy really takes it seriously' (6/22/1958: 58). Leon Weiss also remembers these games since his dad was the pitcher at times. Recalling what he believes were the color of the uniforms, "green and white," Leon also recollects an "ice chest they had on the bench with beer to hydrate the boys on those hot summer days." Whether the games were at Palmer Park on the border between Highland Park and Detroit or at Lahser and 9 mile in Southfield (the suburban city where WXYZ-TV would move its offices in 1959), Soupy would attract an audience, most of whom were too young to partake of the beers in the ice chest.

An interview with Barbara in May of 1958 in the *Detroit News* also probes how Soupy's public persona intrudes on this private life. "As soon as people find out who I am," Barbara explains, "the questions start...They want always to know what it's like to be the wife of a popular television performer...Frankly, it's pretty lonely." As the article points out, "Mrs. Sales see little of her husband during the week." "Even when he's home," Barbara makes clear, "his mind is on the shows." According to the *Detroit News* report, she often offers her feedback on the evening show. "We talk about what I thought about it. I try to be frank on the theory if a man can't get an honest opinion from his wife, whom can he turn to?" (5/12/58: 20).

In his own reminiscences of his father's busy schedule, Tony Sales recalls how Soupy "was doing two shows a day, five days a week and resting the other two. So, we'd come home and have to be real quiet. Then, he'd be out late in the afternoon to do his night show. My brother and I didn't see much of him, because he was working all the time. So, we really didn't get much of a chance to interact with him very much, unless there were some new jokes to be told" (Sales 2001: 84). Soupy's own take on his lack of family interaction was "I didn't spend as much time with my family as I might have...(but) I also had to provide for them, which meant spending time away from them" (Sales 2001:85). That absence may have been one of the reasons for Barbara's filing for divorce in 1960. Under the heading of "Mrs. Soupy Files Suit for Divorce," the *Free Press* news item cites the charge that "her husband preferred to conduct himself as a single man" (5/7/60: 4. Not wanting to speculate on the inclusive meaning of the charge, especially in the absence of complete documentary evidence, it does seem that beyond Soupy's busy show business schedule there may have been some other alleged monkey business. Nonetheless, Soupy and Barbara reconciled later, only to get legally divorced in 1979.)

That separation may have been one of the motivating factors for Soupy to leave Detroit and move to Los Angeles. His own reflections on that move reveal both personal and professional incentives: "I thought it was time I move on because I didn't want to be sixty, sixty-five and be sitting around one night having a drink and wonder if I could have made it in another market. And the timing was right, because I was separated from Barbara and that gave me the freedom to take a chance. After a lot of thought, I approached the people from Jell-O and told them I wanted to move to Los Angeles, and they said I could do the last fifteen shows out there. And so, leaving my family back in Detroit, I packed up and moved myself and my cast of characters to Hollywood, a move that would eventually send my star soaring...at least for a while" (Sales 2001: 85).

Examining what happened to Soupy in Los Angeles and then New York will constitute the next and final chapter in the life and times of this popular television personality. Leaving the place that really launched his television career would, nonetheless, remain a draw for him throughout the rest of his time as a comedic performer. Maybe his continual search for the right medium for a lucrative and successful television livelihood can be explained, in part, by this gag that Soupy used on several occasions: "My next door neighbors are fortune tellers. They told me to turn down my television. I told them I would find a 'happy medium.'" While it will be clear that Soupy sought fame and fortune in the larger markets of LA and New York with mixed results, the television personality that was manufactured and perfected in Detroit would continue to exert its residual effects for the rest of his career.

CHAPTER SEVEN

DETROIT AFTERIMAGES

Although Soupy's move to Los Angeles seemed precipitous to many of his Motor City fans, the relocation for him and the show had been in process for some time. As far back as 1956, Soupy ruminated on the probability of leaving Detroit. In the aftermath of his 1955 network appearance as a summer substitute for *Kukla, Fran and Ollie*, he had been engaged in conversations with ABC executives and New York talent agents about making a move to a larger market like New York or Los Angeles. Still expressing satisfaction with his personal and professional life in Detroit, Soupy, nonetheless, observed in 1956 that "to get anywhere in TV, a performer has to leave Detroit. The sponsors and agencies don't want to spend money to send people here from New York" (*Detroit Free Press* 3/11/1956: 49). It is hardly surprising, therefore, that Hollywood and New York were aspirational attractions for Soupy.

After a number of trips to Los Angeles for screen tests (as early as 1957) and discussions about possible television and movie roles, Soupy landed a small role in 1960 as a cowboy in the TV show, *The Rebel.* Obviously impressed by the extensive production apparatus for this television series, Soupy contrasted his experience on the Hollywood set with his WXYZ-TV operation: "That's one of the tough things about local TV shows. The crew has to do too many things. On my network show we have a hand picked crew because that's a prestige thing, but little local shows don't get that advantage." He further lamented: "We've got to face it here in Detroit. Local live television is dying. WXYZ has been doing more than other stations, but next season the network is taking over more time and there'll be fewer jobs" (*Detroit Free Press* 7/31/1960: TV 3). Having lost his evening program, *Soupy's On*, at the end of 1959 and having his daily noontime show moved to a morning time slot by WXYZ-TV, Soupy could see the writing on the wall even if it did not appear written out on the blackboard as either "Words of Wisdom" or "Soupy Sez."

After negotiating with ABC TV to continue the Saturday *Lunch with Soupy Sales* through the winter of 1961, Soupy brought with him from Detroit some key members of that noontime program. This included the puppet master, Clyde Adler, the director Bill Carruthers, and a select group of others affiliated with his lunchtime show. When the syndicated Saturday program ended on March 25, 1961, a local version of the show was already airing on KABC-TV Los Angeles on weekdays in the early evening. With solid ratings for the KABC program, ABC decided to do a syndicated telecast of *The Soupy Sales Show* on Friday evening from 7:30-8:00 P.M., starting on January 26, 1962. Although the budget and crew were bigger with a more elaborate set and scripted sketches, the show was cancelled after twelve weeks (Sales 2001: 91 and 94).

However, during those few months of the evening network program, Soupy attracted some Hollywood celebrities whose guest appearances on *The Soupy Sales Show* would primarily consist of getting hit in the face with a pie. Among those celebrities was Frank Sinatra. Both Soupy and Sinatra got a pie in their face after opening the door and claiming it was Dean Martin who was the hit man (Sales 2001: 93-4). Other Hollywood actors clamored to be on the show just to get hit with a pie.

Burt Lancaster demanded a pie in the face so he could be a "hero" to his children, especially since, according to Lancaster, they were "avid fans" of Soupy's evening program (Grossman 1987: 128). That appearance was taped, as Soupy observes, "so he (Lancaster) could be home, watching TV with his kids and seeing the surprise on their faces when they saw him walk out" (Sales 2001: 94). Tony Curtis, another Hollywood actor and celebrity, also came on the program as a "surprise to his kids" (Sales 2001: 94). But there was one "celebrity" who managed to avoid getting hit in the face with a pie when she turned up on the show. As a canine guest, Lassie apparently was exempt from being pummeled with the aerosol fluff. The photograph of Soupy shaking Lassie's paw in his memoir is accompanied with the following note: "They wanted me to hit Lassie with a pie...I decided to shake hands instead" (Sales 2001: 105).

With Hollywood celebrities becoming regulars on Soupy's LA show, the pie-in-the-face became the defining feature for his guests and his audience. As a consequence Soupy's own celebrity status grew while the very defining characteristics of his Detroit television personality – authenticity, ordinariness, and typicality – tended to fade. As Joshua Gamson notes, celebrity defers authenticity as "superficial fragments (such as pies-in-the-face) circulate" (1994: 196). Although there were still residual markings from Soupy's Motor City manufactured comedic style, the Motor City was, itself, undergoing transformations as a consequence of continuing deindustrialization. During Soupy's time in LA, Motown replaced the Motor City as a culturally resonant moniker for Detroit (Maraniss 2015; and Smith 1999. Motown, that manufactured musical empire spawned by Berry Gordy, would abandon Detroit for LA in the early 1970s.)

Soupy and Frank Sinatra Get Hit with pies

Besides all the pies that were launched at the faces of Hollywood celebrities during the 1962 network show, Soupy managed to record his second record album. After a 1961 release of the first record album, *The Soupy Sales Show*, gained some critical and popular recognition, the second one, *Up in the Air,* continued the format of exchanges with all the regular puppets. With Soupy playing his typical role of interlocutor, especially with White Fang, one of those exchanges was in response to White Fang's apparent objection to not receiving a big enough introduction. Soupy's response to the "Araaah-araah-araah" from White Fang, was: "Here's a dog whose sounds will go to your head and to your heart – and they aren't going to do your stomach any good either' (Sales 2001: 102).

Another routine with White Fang seems particularly relevant to Soupy's transition from Los Angeles to New York: *White Fang: Raah-oh-raah-oh-raah./Soupy: What's that you say, White Fang, Paramount keeps calling you about shorts?/White Fang: Raah./Did you leave your shorts at the Paramount Theater again?* As on numerous occasions in Detroit, LA, and New York, White Fang's answer comes in the form of a pie in Soupy's face (Sales 2001: 108).

White Fang was joined in this assault on Soupy's television visage by KABC- TV, but without the comedic relief. Following a conflict with the station management, Soupy's local show was cancelled in favor of running other syndicated programs. So, to support his wife and two sons, Soupy turned to doing as many personal appearances and guest spots as possible. In one of his few guest spots on a television series during this time in Los Angeles, Soupy got to play himself on the CBS sit-com, *Hennesy.* Lieutenant Hennesy, a Navy dentist played by the former child actor, Jackie Cooper, invited Soupy to entertain the child patients at a naval hospital (Sales 2001: 233). Apparently, with the exception of a guest spot as the host of the *Tonight Show*, there were very few other invitations and engagements beyond these television appearances. Therefore, unable to secure permanent employment in the entertainment business in Los Angeles, he had to look elsewhere. Fortunately, that elsewhere was New York (Sales 2001: 109-10).

Offered a gig on WNEW-TV in 1964, Soupy moved his family to the Big Apple. Although Clyde Adler remained behind in Los Angeles, Soupy contacted Frank Nastasi, who was in New York pursuing his acting career, to take over for Clyde. Essentially replicating the format of the prior shows in Los Angeles and Detroit, Soupy and Frank began a half hour show to be aired weekdays on 5:00 P.M. called *The Soupy Sales Show*. Eschewing the cockeyed top hat and big bowtie from his

Detroit days for a regular-sized bowtie, sweater, and bare head, Soupy would, nonetheless, build on the zany and even Dadaesque comedy routines honed during his time in the Motor City (Greene 2008: 85-95). Among the new sketch comedy routines that Soupy created were two that would be particular favorites for him, his crew and cast, and the New York audience. As a parody of TV crime shows, "The Adventures of Philo Kvetch" starred Soupy in the role of Kvetch, a clumsy police investigator whose prime mission is to seek out and arrest a notorious crime figure known as the "Mask." Not only did Frank Nastasi play the Mask, but he also performed the roles of Onions Oregano, a hitman for the Mask, and Bruno the Killer Ape (Sales 2001: 234). The popularity of the sketch allowed Soupy to film on location around New York and add a number of guest stars to expand the total number of episodes to thirty-nine (Sales 2001: 153).

Another sketch routine involved welcoming guests to an ersatz French restaurant, known as "Chez Bippy." According to one of the disc jockeys on WNEW radio who performed as one of those guests, he appeared in a "top hat and tails," only to be eventually smashed in the face with a pie after causing a "ruckus in the place" (Sales 2001: 117). Chez Bippy would also be a site for a reprise for Frank Sinatra. Bringing along some of his "rat pack," (Sammy Davis and Trini Lopez) Sinatra, once again, became the recipient of an aerosol pie. Soupy estimated that the number of pies tossed around in that particular episode was close to two hundred (Sales 2001: 124-25).

The slapstick humor and pies galore, especially because of the guest stars involved, attracted both kids and adults, resulting in enhancing Soupy's New York television personality even as it absorbed the comedic template manufactured in Detroit. A 1965 article in the New York *Hearld Tribune*, under the title of "Love in the Afternoon," examined that attraction to Soupy's show: "To begin with, Soupy is funny. He entertains. The kids like the bits, the mugging, the routines. The parents like the one-liners, the hip references and the air of controlled hysteria...it is the essence of live television and therefore a rarity" (Newman and Benton 1965: 7). As Frank Nastasi recalls, "the kids watched us because they loved the pie bits and the falls and all that slapstick kind of stuff...But the adults loved us because some of the performers who came on the show." Those performers included vocal groups like the Supremes, Ronnie Spector, and Judy Collins. There were also well-known comedians who appeared on the show, such as Jack Leonard, Nipsey Russell, and Henny Youngman (Sales 2001: 130).

But it was Soupy's own antics that drew the audience to the show, often creating iconic moments that resonated beyond the momentary flashes on the screen. One of those moments is best described by Soupy since it went on to become the Grammy award-winning record called "The Mouse:" "I was always coming up with all kinds of silly dances...and for one of them I put my fingers to my ears and started wiggling them and called it 'The Mouse' which was a takeoff I'd dreamed up on 'The Monkey' and other teen dance crazes of the time...Well, it caught on – I did a recording of the song – and it kind of went through the roof. In New York, they sold a quarter of a million copes in one week" (Sales 2001: 150). Given the media market in the New York area, it is hardly surprising that Soupy's dance *shtick*, drawing from his Detroit shuffle, would attract such an adoring teenage audience, already primed by the music industry to seek out a new dance craze.

Soupy's promotion for the Hit Song and Dance, The Mouse

As a consequence of Soupy's television and record performances, he developed a fanatically loyal following among those New York teenagers who watched the show on WNEW-TV. Because of his popularity, Soupy was invited to make personal appearances all around the city. A few of those did not go as smoothly as planned. One of the public events at a department store in Queens almost resulted in a riot when hundreds of kids overwhelmed the security guards and pursued Soupy for an autograph. Less threatening to Soupy, but nearly as tumultuous because of the crowd size and some snafu, was his invitation from Macy's to be part of the Thanksgiving Day parade in 1965 (Sales 2001: 129 and 126). Somehow, that well-run New York department store misplaced the float on which Soupy was to ride, leaving him, instead, "sitting on the hood of a black limousine" (Newman and Benton 1965: 8).

Earlier that year in mid-April, Soupy did a ten-day stint at the Paramount Theatre as part of a variety concert billed as *Soupy Sales Easter Show*. Since it also overlapped with Passover, there was some concern about whether it would attract any customers. It broke box office records with throngs of teenagers jamming each show and "mounted police all over the place." The performers on the bill included Little Richard, whose guitar player at the time was the then obscure Jimi Hendrix, the Hollies with Graham Nash, the singer Shirley Ellis, whose big hit was "The Name Game," a group of dancers, and the King Curtis Band. (Sales 2001: 145).

The crazed crowds following Soupy may very well be attributed, in part, to a rather notorious incident that occurred on New Year's Day in 1965, resulting in Soupy's subsequent suspension by WNEW-TV. Because of its notoriety, he has recounted what transpired on the last few minutes of his January 1, 1965 show on many different occasions and in a wide variety of venues. Since Frank Nastasi was there that day as part of the smaller holiday staff, his perspective on what happened warrants consideration. As Nastasi tells it, there was a minute or two left on the show. Looking directly into the camera, as he so often did, Soupy directed the "gang" to "go into your mom and pop's room and go into their pants and pocketbooks and get me the pieces of paper with George Washington's picture on it. Send it to me and I'll send you a picture postcard from Puerto Rico." Continuing with his narrative about the repercussions, Nastasi asserts "all hell broke loose when some lady complained that we were preaching to kids on how to rob. We were suspended for ten days, Soupy without pay, and me, suspended with pay. But suddenly and believe me, we never could have predicted this would happen, we were heroes. The people, mostly college kids, came and picketed the studio, yelling things like, 'Freedom of Speech' and all that" (Sales 2001: 140-41).

Because of the protests, Soupy returned to the show. Still, there was a reckoning with the fallout from Soupy's New Year's Day pitch to kids. According to Soupy, notwithstanding his embellishments, he took in around $80,000, "all in Monopoly money or fake cash." The "one-dollar" he did receive he deposited "into some fund-raising canister outside the station" (Grossman 1987: 128). To say the least, management was not happy with any of his or his fans antics in the matter. "When I returned after my suspension," Soupy recounts, "things weren't much better at the station because every time I turned around I was fighting with them. Often, it was about the budget. It was like pulling teeth from a chicken, and chickens don't have any teeth." In spite of these difficulties with management and the opprobrium some critics heaped on him for this and other gags, Soupy realized that his fans more than made up for "the aggravation" he suffered through their acts of loyalty (Sales 2001: 139 and 145).

While that loyalty helped to build the success of *The Soupy Sales Show*, resulting by 1966 in syndication to over fifty television markets in the United States and to several different English-speaking countries, the conflicts that Soupy had with management led him to refuse to continue beyond 1966. Although there is some dispute about the termination of Soupy's contract, it was evident to those working with him, such as Art Seidel, one of the producers of the program, that both Soupy and management were exhausted by the conflicts at the station. "I think the show could have run quite a while," notes Seidel. "It was probably a combination of Soupy being tired of fighting with management and it was a constant struggle. I think what it goes back to is that the station didn't really recognize what they had" (Sales 2001: 162).

If WNEW-TV executives didn't comprehend the comic treasure that Soupy represented, there were certainly others who were more than willing to hire Soupy for their own television shows. Indeed, the TV game show producer, Bob Stewart, who hired Soupy as a regular on *What's My Line* (from 1968-1974) and other television game programs after that, recognized Soupy's affinity for the format: "Soupy has always been a natural for a celebrity game show, because they're free form and put people in a perfect ad-lib situation. Soupy would give us not only a celebrity with the skill of playing the game, but also the persona of a very funny man. Someone like Soupy is much funnier than a straight actor, and besides being bright and good at all the games, Soupy always entertained" (Sales 2001: 165). While Stewart identifies Soupy as a "celebrity," it is important to note that such a designation contains numerous contradictions as Graeme Turner underscores in his *Understanding Celebrity* (2004). In particular,

Soupy retained the qualities of his manufactured television personality – ordinary, familiar, and authentic - throughout his career.

Of course, Soupy did not stop entertaining throughout most of the latter part of the twentieth century until an accident in 1995 and subsequent failing health cut short his non-stop pace. Whether as a panelist on various game shows, a regular on the syndicated 1976-1981 *Sha Na Na* TV program, initially appearing as a police jester and then as "Igor," the attendant of the Sha Na Na Clubhouse, a special guest on any number of variety shows, bit parts in films and television, the reprise of his old format in 1979 for *The New Soupy Sales Show* (shot in Los Angeles with Clyde Adler being flown in from Michigan), and various nightclub gigs, Soupy demonstrated his comedic chops (Sales 2001: 235-39). He even managed to secure a spot on WNBC-AM radio, sandwiched in between Howard Stern and Don Imus, from 1984 to 1988. Unlike Stern and Imus who had a reputation for raunchy and off-color remarks, Soupy, according to one of his regular guests, "was never off-color or offensive. (He) was always so gracious to his crew, listeners, and guests" (Sales 2001: 217. On the other hand, a number of my interviewees reported seeing him do "off-color", "adult," or "blue" material during his gigs as a stand-up comedian in various venues in the metro Detroit area during the 1970s and 1980s).

In order to develop the format for the radio show, Soupy took on a co-writer, Ray D'ariano. D'ariano recalls "the concept of the show included band music similar to that used on *The Tonight Show*, and sound effects like applause. It was going to be kind of like Theatre of the Mind, but on radio. The picture listeners were supposed to get was of Soupy on the couch with his sidekick, me, and the orchestra was over there, and the audience was over here, kind of thing." From Soupy's perspective the radio program constituted a "variety talk show... kind of a throwback to the earlier days of radio." Soupy's take on that variety talk show was "I'd do a monologue. I'd play music. I'd do interviews. I'd take phone calls. We'd do the news, weather, and traffic reports, of course. And I'd have a stable of funny characters... that would appear regularly on the show" (Sales 2001: 209 and 207).

Soupy did not have to rely on a "stable of funny characters" for his periodic appearances in Detroit during the 1970s, 1980s, and into the 1990s. A number of my interviewees recall seeing Soupy in the 1980s and 1990s in various clubs in the metro Detroit area. As Suzanne Paul recollects, "I saw him at The Holly Inn in Holly, Michigan (a town north of Detroit). He was doing stand up and he was great." Commenting on his earlier return to the Detroit area for a gig in 1971 at Top-Hat Supper Club just across the border in Windsor, columnist Susan Holmes considered his last decade of ups and downs in the entertainment industry. "Time after time since leaving Detroit," she writes, "Soupy has teetered on the fine edge of success in network television as something other than a kiddie star. And each time, success has been as close and elusive as a sunbeam slipping through a child's fingers." Quoting Soupy on that elusive success, he observes, "I realize I've done 20 times better and I'm making 20 times more than an awful lot of people who have been in the business as long as I have" (*Detroit Free Press* 7/11/1971: 6B).

On another revisit to Detroit two years later, the *Free Press* entertainment columnist, Lawrence DeVine, followed Soupy into a northside restaurant, acknowledging that Soupy had "once again" displayed his status as "the Pied Piper of Detroit. If a new generation of television-watchers do not know the old-time pie thrower, the elder fans still do. His return was reunion time. Waitresses giggled when he put his autograph on paper napkins and he whispered, 'Don't cash this until Thursday. I'm a little short.'" When one of those waitresses brought him a Bloody Mary, "Soupy noisily sucked on the celery stalk in his Bloody Mary (complaining) there's something wrong with this straw." The waitress then inquired, "Soupy when are you coming back? I won't tell you how old I am, but I used to watch you every day as a kid" (2/8/1973: 14D).

Soupy, of course, could not avoid coming back to the place where he had so many fans. Bob Talbert's 1979 column in the *Free Press* was another example of that fandom. Under the heading of "Soupy Sales still No. 1 to many of us," Talbert highlighted Soupy's annual participation in a telethon bearing his name for mentally challenged kids. "Once a year since 1973," Talbert writes, "Soupy has put on his telethon to raise the bulk of the money for distribution to (agencies dealing with those afflicted with childhood cognitive impairments)." While Talbert identifies the Johnny Trudell orchestra as the musical entertainment, my friend and local jazz musician, Bill Meyer, also performed from 1973 to 1979 at the Light Guard Armory on the northern border of Detroit. Bill's memory of those gigs in the late hours of the telethon revealed his appreciation for the kind of "jazz comedy" that Soupy represented to him and so many other Detroiters, an improvisational style whose comedic riffs were punctuated by punch line after punch line.

When Soupy came back, once again in 1986, for a Children's Hospital benefit, it was as an honoree for all the times he had performed for kids at the hospital during his residence in Detroit in the 1950s. Soupy was also being recognized for his vanguard role in "network children's programming during his years on Detroit's Channel 7 in the 1950s." When asked about the present standing of children's programming, he responded, "It's abominable. There's not one show besides *Sesame Street* with a live role model – someone telling kids to eat their vegetables and not talk to strangers. All the cartoons are violent and the soaps are soft-core porn" (Craig in *Free Press* 1/19/1986: 3L).

While Soupy may not have been remembered by most of his Detroit fans as a role model, he was a happy memory for so many of those viewers of his WXYZ-TV daytime and evening shows. He also continued to exert a tremendous nostalgia for his comedic craziness as attested to by my interviewees and by those extensive commentaries posted online about those old Soupy Sales programs. He was, indeed, a legendary and lasting television personality, manufactured, for the most part, in Detroit. On one of Soupy's final trips back to Detroit for a promotion of the A&E telecast of his biography, the *Free Press* television columnist, Mike Duffy, declared, "Soupy was – and remains – slapstick *sui generis...(*He) is a downright illustrious hall-of-fame television institution" (12/21/1994: 7D).

Examining Soupy's legacy, particularly, but not exclusively, in the context of his television time in the Motor City will provide the necessary tribute and conclusion to this book.

CONCLUSION

Looking back on his experiences in Detroit during an interview conducted by Charles Salzberg, the co-author of the Sales's memoir, Soupy acknowledges "even today more than forty years later, there still exists a great love between me and the Motor City. I go back there at least a couple of times a year, and I'm still amazed at the wonderful reaction I get" (Sales 2001: 84). As he observed in an earlier question-and-answer session conducted in 1994 by Carol Teegarden for the *Detroit Free Press*, "Detroit was the best thing that ever happened to me" (9/28/1994: 6C). Although possibly marred by hyperbole, there is no denying either the affection shown by Detroiters for Soupy or the significance that his time on WXYZ-TV had for his career as a television personality.

The connection established between Soupy Sales and his Motor City fans and viewers was as much a testament to who he was as a television personality as to the temper of the times when he reigned as a preeminent local celebrity. As Detroit television historian, Tim Kiska, contends, "it was a different time in television. People expected a whole lot less from the medium. There was much less pressure to perform. You could walk in and say, 'let's try this today,' and you could get away with it. There was a certain spontaneity around... that was a big deal" (Quoted in O'Connell 2008: 15). There is no doubt about the role that spontaneity played in Soupy's noontime show. Beyond the slapstick routines, the funny gags, and the pies in the face, the atmosphere of casualness and silliness created an authentic rapport between Soupy, his crew and the viewing audience.

The relaxed environment on the lunchtime program reinforced the sense that Soupy Sales was an intimate member of the family who brought relief to kids and adults in fraught times. The pressures to conform either on the job or in school, along with economic uncertainties and social and political injustices that obtained during the 1950s in the Motor City and beyond (from Cold War repression to racial discrimination), could be cast aside during a brief half hour of ridiculous hilarity with Soupy. As Bob Talbert, a *Detroit Free Press* entertainment columnist, points out: "People thought of him as one of themselves. He was a star, yes, but he was an approachable star. He had that homey quality that people identified with" (Sales 2001: 130). Indeed, it was that televisual connection of approachability and familiarity that boosted Soupy's star and gave him a tremendous celebrity status in the Motor City.

Nevertheless, for most kids watching Soupy's daytime programs the immediate bond was the irreverence of his humor. Mary Wilson, one of the members of the Motown legendary group, The Supremes, recollected, "I always, as a kid, thought Soupy Sales was the funniest guy on this earth. He always had pies thrown in his face, and at the time I thought that was very hilarious. He was definitely my favorite person on TV" (Castelnero 2009: 11). Growing up in the nearby suburb of Royal Oak, Frank Joyce cited Soupy's "irreverence" as the main draw to his humor and an inspiration for the publication at his high school of *The Daily Smirker*, a "forerunner of the underground press" that he and some others, including Tom Hayden, Dondero grad and sixties radical, produced (Mast 1994: 276).

While it may stretch credulity to suggest that Soupy Sales was a major motivation for the dissident activism of the 1960s, that irreverent attitude that pervaded many of the bits on the noontime show did contribute to a generational reaction against a stultifying status quo. One historian of comedy cites Soupy, along with other forms of impertinent humor, as influential in shaping the attitudes of the Baby Boomers. "Our generation," George Stewart observes, "had a few major influences. One of them was *MAD* magazine. The absurdist kind of humor is why, I think, we wound up not trusting the government, or taking everything with a grain of salt. Some people think that people of my generation are way too cynical. I just think we have a realistic view of things. I think...that jaundiced eye comes from comedians like Soupy Sales and Ernie Kovacs and *MAD* magazine" (Quoted in O'Connell 2008: 15. Emerging in 1952 as a small comic book, *MAD* transformed into a magazine in 1955 and gained increasing popularity. By 1958 *MAD* had 1.3 million readers. I was among them, especially delighting in the parodies and satires of the dominant popular and political culture. For a history of *MAD*, see Reidelbach 1991.). As an indication of the validity of this perspective, practically all of my interviewees agreed that Soupy's humor had an impact on how they look at the world through similar comedic lenses that, as one of them acknowledged, indicated an "absurd sense of humor."

For some of those who watched *Lunch with Soupy Sales*, the bond that was forged had much more to do with a sense of intimate familiarity than with the madcap comedy. One commentary that appeared on the internet about Soupy's show reveals the effect of his ability to connect in a comforting way: "When I was a little girl in Detroit, during the 50s, I was very lonely. My father was an alcoholic, my mother took prescription drugs. They were so involved with their own problems. I was alone most of the time. I would run home for lunch every day to eat with Soupy Sales. It was like having lunch every day with a friend. I never met him, but I want to thank him for all those lunches I didn't have to eat alone" (Sales 2001: 229). Although her own situation was not representative of the kids who ate lunch with Soupy since most of them, reflective of the gender dynamics of the period, had stay-at-home moms, her feeling of having a "friend" for her noontime meal was very indicative of how thankful so many others, including all of my interviewees, were for Soupy's companionship.

Soupy's demeanor on his evening show, *Soupy's On*, and in his personal appearances conveyed a respect for his guests, the television audience, his fans, and the public at large. Because of his great love of jazz and his obvious admiration for the legendary jazz musicians who performed for *Soupy's On*, it may not be a stretch to say that he helped to counter the lingering and invidious racism that informed the institutions and attitudes still prevalent in Detroit and across the United States. This earnest side of Soupy, however, did not sacrifice the comedy in sketch routines on the evening show or off-hand remarks to the crew and studio musicians. (Joe Messina recounts how Soupy would tease him by saying something to the effect that if Joe didn't stop picking at the guitar, it would never heal.) Indeed, Soupy manifested, at the same time, a serious demeanor when introducing his musical guests and jester-like behavior when performing the countless sketch comedy bits on the evening show. On the one hand, if it had not been for pressure from ABC-TV network executives to cancel the evening show in favor of the standard news show at 11 pm, Soupy might have continued with *Soupy's On* (Osgood 1981:374). On the other hand, Soupy and many of the local jazz musicians were in the process of seeking better career opportunities elsewhere.

Nonetheless, his personal appearances during his seven years on WXYZ-TV, also, demonstrated a wide-ranging commitment to entertain his fans and the public, irrespective of the size or nature of the venue and audience. Those appearances, a mix of his own loyalty to the fans, his self-promotion, and the publicity by Channel 7, manufactured a well-regarded television personality whose achievements went beyond his formative years in Detroit during the 1950s. Therefore, it might be appropriate to conclude this book with slight revision of one of the jokes that Soupy included in his book, *Stop Me If You've Heard It!*:

> *Two men are sitting at a bar, really enjoying each other's company. They're drinking and talking baseball, music, comedy, and exchanging gags. They pay the check and they agree to meet in the same bar at the same time, ten years later.*
>
> *Ten years later one of them walks into the bar a little skeptical, and, sure enough, there's his pal sitting on a stool. The guy hurries over to his friend and says, "I never thought that day when I walked out of this bar ten years ago that I'd really see you here ten years later? So when did you get back here?"*
>
> *And his friend looks at him and says, "Back? Who left?"* (Sales 2003: 125).

While Soupy physically left us in 2009, he really has never left as a presence in our lives. Even if Soupy, in the words of the immortal Bard, "shuffled off his mortal coil" (doing the Soupy Shuffle all the way), his spirit is alive and well. It resides in the vivid memories so many of us Soupy fans retain. It inhabits the videos that remain extant on YouTube and other websites. Considering the influence Soupy exerted on kids in Detroit during the 1950s, it is instructive that a number of Detroit-based television commentators referred to him as a "pied piper." In that regard, if no longer around as a physical television personality, his spectral image beckons us to follow where he leads.

APPENDIX A

QUESTIONNAIRE ON SOUPY SALES'S SHOWS ON WXYZ-TV, 1953-1960

You are receiving this form because you indicated a willingness to respond to questions about your viewing of any or all of the programs featuring Soupy Sales that aired on WXYZ-TV from 1953-1960. Because there are only a few tapes that remain of these shows, I am relying on your memories to help me reconstruct the content of these programs. In addition, your responses may help identify what impact those shows had on you, as well as other connections you may have had to Soupy's time in Metro Detroit. I hope to use these questionnaires as critical input for my projected book. If you wish to be quoted for the projected book, please provide your signature at the bottom with a telephone number. Thank you.

Francis Shor, Emeritus Professor, History, Wayne State University

(Please use the back if you need more space for your answers)

1. NAME: (leave blank if you wish to remain anonymous): Birth Date:

2. AGES FROM 1953-1960:

3. WHERE YOU RESIDED FROM 1953-1960:

4. WHICH SCHOOLS DID YOU ATTEND AND FOR WHAT GRADES:

5. WHAT DID YOU PARENTS DO:

6. DID YOUR FAMILY OWN A TV, WHAT KIND & WHERE WAS IT LOCATED:

7. HOW MANY HOURS A DAY AND WEEK DID YOU WATCH TV:

8. WHICH SOUPY SALES'S SHOWS DID YOU WATCH IN WHAT YEARS:

>   MORNING PROGRAM (8 am):

>   LUNCH PROGRAM (first called "12 o'clock Comics", then "Lunch with Soupy"):

>   EVENING PROGRAM ("Soupy's On" at 11 pm) – Can you recall any guests and what they did?:

9. WHAT CHARACTERS WERE MOST MEMORABLE AND WHY?

10. WHAT SKITS AND/OR JOKES DO YOU REMEMBER?

11. WHAT SPONSORS OF HIS SHOWS DO YOU REMEMBER:

12. DID YOUR FRIENDS WATCH? IF SO, WHAT WAS THE FOCUS OF YOUR DISCUSSION OF THESE "SOUPY" SHOWS?

13. WHAT OTHER TV PROGRAMS DID YOU WATCH DURING THIS PERIOD? DO YOU REMEMBER WHICH CHANNEL THEY WERE ON? HOW DID THEY COMPARE TO SOUPY'S SHOWS?

14. DID YOU EVER SEE SOUPY AT PUBLIC APPEARANCES – WHERE AND WHEN?

15. WHAT KIND OF IMPACT DID SOUPY HAVE, IF ANY, ON YOUR SENSE OF HUMOR, OR ON YOUR PERSONALITY?

16. FOR JEWISH RESPONDENTS ONLY: IN WHAT WAYS, IF ANY, DID SOUPY RELATE TO YOUR JEWISH IDENTITY AND THAT OF YOUR FAMILY AND FRIENDS?

17. ANY OTHER COMMENTS YOU WISH TO MAKE (use the back if necessary):

18. SIGNATURE/DATE/TELEPHONE:

PLEASE RETURN THIS COMPLETED QUESTIONNAIRE TO FRAN SHOR EITHER BY EMAIL: f.shor@wayne.edu or by snail mail at 703 Washington Place Dr., Royal Oak, MI 48067

I put together the above questionnaire after some preliminary discussion with friends who were lifelong Detroiters and fans of Soupy Sales, keeping in mind the specific subjects to be addressed in the book. In order to disseminate the questionnaire, I posted a note on my Facebook page and the Jewish Life in Detroit FB page soliciting email addresses for those Detroiters who watched Soupy Sales during the 1950s. My wife's cousin, Ricky Stoler, a lifelong Detroiter, put out a notification on his extensive email list for Soupy Sales fans to contact me if they wished to fill out the questionnaire. Because this list was dominated by his Jewish contacts, the number of Jewish respondents among the final two-dozen was over-representative of the actual percentage of Jews in the Metro Detroit area during the 1950s. Of the twenty-four respondents, eight were Jewish. While this percentage was almost ten times greater than the actual Jewish population at the time, skewing the questionnaire's demographics, those responses and follow-up interviews, nonetheless, provided important material related to Soupy's Jewish identity, what constituted Jewish humor, etc.

As far as the other demographics, there were twice as many male as female respondents (16 to 8). Since only two of the respondents were Black, they were underrepresented of the growing Black population of Detroit during the 1950s as it went from about eighteen to twenty-five percent in the ten-year period. Baby boomers outnumbered those born before 1946 by two to one (16 to 8). Only four of the respondents lived outside the city.

APPENDIX B

SOUPY'S WXYZ-TV SHOWS (1953-1960)

Program/Name	Dates (Debut & Demise)	Time (Days & Duration)	Format
12 O'Clock Comics	April 6, 1953–October 10, 1958	Noon—Mon–Fri—30 minutes (11:45am start in winter 1958)	cartoons, films, puppets
Soupy's On	September 28, 1953–November 27, 1959	11pm— Mon–Fri—10 & 15 minutes (30 minutes, starting November 1956)	music, variety, skits
Soupy's Ranch	May 26, 1954–July 21, 1954	7pm—Wed—60 minutes	Cowboy films
Soupy Sales Show	July 4, 1955–August 26, 1955	6pm—Mon–Fri—30 minutes (ABC syndication)	cartoons, puppets
Breakfasttime with Soupy	October 13, 1958–November 28, 1960	7:30am— Mon–Fri—60 minutes 7:00 am – Mon-Fri – 60 minutes	cartoons, puppets
Lunch with Soupy Sales	October 3, 1959–December 1960	Noon—Sat—30 minutes (ABC syndication)	cartoons, films, puppets

BIBLIOGRAPHY

Anonymous. 1954. "Tension." *Correspondence.* Subscription Special. In Martin Glaberman Papers, Box 10:2, Walter Reuther Archives, Wayne State University.

Appy, Christian. 2015. *American Reckoning: The Vietnam War and National Identity.* New York: Viking.

Babson, Steve, Dave Riddle, and David Elsila. 2010. *The Color of Law: Ernie Goodman and the Struggle for Labor and Civil Rights.* Detroit, MI.: Wayne State University Press.

Bariaud, Francoise. 1988. "Age Differences in Children's Humor." In *Humor and Children's Development: A Guide to Practical Applications,* edited by Paul E. McGhee, 15-45. New York: The Hayworth Press.

Bennett, James. 2011. *Television Personalities: Stardom and the Small Screen.* New York: Routledge.

Berger, Arthur Asa. 2001. *Jewish Jesters: A Study in American Popular Comedy.* Cresskill, N.J: Hampton Press.

Berman, Lila. 2015. *Metropolitan Jews: Politics, Race, and Religion in Postwar Detroit.* Chicago: The University of Chicago Press.

Bjorn, Lars (with Jim Gallert). 2004. *Before Motown: A History of Jazz in Detroit.* Ann Arbor: The University of Michigan Press.

Boddy, William. 1990. *Television: Its Industry and its Critics.* Urbana: University of Illinois Press.

Boggs, Grace Lee. 1998. *Living for Change: An Autobiography.* Minneapolis: University of Minnesota Press.

Boorstin, Daniel. 1961. *The Image: A Guide to Pseudo-Events in America.* New York: Harper & Row.

Boyd, Robert. 1957. "Soupy's Gang Frolics with Scripts or Not." *Detroit Free Press,* November 17, 1957: 14 TV.

Castelnero, Gordon. 2009. *TV Land Detroit.* Ann Arbor: University of Michigan Press.

Clark, Daniel. 2018. *Disruption in Detroit: Autoworkers and the Elusive Postwar Boom.* Urbana: University of Illinois Press.

Cook, Louis. 1955. "10,000 Little 'Davy Crocketts' Welcome Their Idol to Detroit." *Detroit Free Press,* June 14, 1955: 3.

Coontz, Stephanie. 2000. *The Way We Never Were: American Families and the Nostalgia Trap.* New York: Basic Books.

Cotter, Bill. 1997. *The Wonderful World of Disney Television.* New York: Hyperion.

Craig, Charlotte W. "Funny Guy Sales Gets Serious About Hospital Benefit." *Detroit Free Press,* January 19, 1986: 3L.

Davis, Miles (with Quincy Troupe). 2011. *The Autobiography of Miles Davis.* New York: Simon & Schuster.

DeBacker, Charlotte J. S. 2012. "Blinded by Starlight: An Evolutionary Framework for Studying Celebrity Culture and Fandom." *Review of General Psychology* 16:2 (June): 144-51.

DesRochers, Rick. 2014. *The Comic Offense from Vaudeville to Contemporary Comedy.* New York: Bloomsbury.

DeVine, Lawrence. 1973. "He's Back! We Love You Soupy, Oh Yes We Do." *Detroit Free Press,* February 8, 1973: 14D.

Duffett, Mark. 2013. *Understanding Fandom.* New York: Bloomsbury Academy.

Duffy, Mike. 1994. "A&E Bio Shows Why Soupy Sells." *Detroit Free Press,* December 21, 1994: 7D.

Englehardt, Tom. 1986. "The Shortcake Strategy." In *Watching Television,* edited by Todd Gitlin, 68-110. New York: Pantheon Books.

Epstein, Lawrence. 2001. *The Haunted Smile: The Story of Jewish Comedians in America.* New York: Public Affairs.

Fiske, John. 2011. *Television Culture,* second edition. New York: Routledge.

Gamson, Joshua. 1994. *Claims to Fame: Celebrity in Contemporary America.* Berkeley, CA: University of California Press.

Golick, Edward. Jr. 2009. "Soupy's On: The Story of Soupy Sales' Late Night Variety Show." http://www.detroitkidshow.com/soupys_on.htm.

Gordon, Linda. 2017. *The Second Coming of the KKK: The Ku Klux Klan of the 1920s and the American Political Tradition.* New York: Liveright Publishing Co.

Greene, Doyle. 2008. *Politics and the American Television Comedy.* Jefferson, N.C.: McFarland & Co.

Grieve, Victoria. 2018. *Little Cold Warriors: American Childhood in the 1950s.* New York: Oxford University Press.

Grossman, Gary H. 1987. *Saturday Morning TV.* New York: Arlington House.

Harris, Sydney. 1956. "Harris Praises Youth, Assails Delinquent Society." *Detroit Free Press*, April 23, 1956: 1.

Hilmes, Michele. 2014. *Only Connect: A Cultural History of Broadcasting in the United States*, fourth edition. Boston: Wadsworth.

Holmes, Susan. 1971. "Now, the Star of Daytime TV: Soupy Sales." *Detroit Free Press*, July 11, 1971: 6B.

Johnson, Arthur L. 2008. *Race and Remembrance*. Detroit, MI: Wayne State University Press.

Jones, LeRoi (Amiri Baraka). 1967. *Blues People*. New York: William Morrow & Co.

Kelley, Robin. D. G. 2010. *Thelonious Monk: The Life and Times of an American Original*. New York: Free Press.

Kiska, Tim. 2001. "The Crazy Days of Soupy Sales." *Detroit News*, October 30, 2001.

Kiska, Tim. 2005. *From Soupy to Nuts: A History of Detroit Television*. Royal Oak, MI.: Momentum Books.

Kordas, Ann Marie. 2013. *The Politics of Childhood in Cold War America*. Brookfield, VT: Pickering & Chatto.

Lipsitz, George. 1990. *Time Passages: Collective Memory and American Popular Culture*. Minneapolis: University of Minnesota Press.

Luke, Carmen. 1990. *Constructing the Child Viewer: A History of the American Discourse on Television and Children, 1950-1980*. New York: Praeger.

Macias, Anthony. 2010. "Detroit Was Heavy: Modern Jazz, Bebop, and African American Expressive Culture." *The Journal of African American History* 95:1 (Winter): 44-70.

MacLean, Nancy. 1994. *Behind the Mask of Chivalry: The Making of The Second Ku Klux Klan*. New York: Oxford University Press.

MacPherson, Myra. 1957. "Soupy Tells Why Kids Love Him." *Detroit Free Press*, August 11, 1957: TV11.

Maraniss, David. 2016. *Once a Great City: A Detroit Story*. New York: Simon & Schuster.

Marc, David. 1997. *Comic Visions: Television Comedy and American Culture*, second edition. Malden, MA: Blackwell.

Marling, Karal Ann. 1994. *As Seen on TV: The Personal Culture of Everyday Life in the 1950s*. Cambridge, MA: Harvard University Press.

Mast, Robert H., ed. 1994. *Detroit Lives*. Philadelphia, PA: Temple University Press.

May, Elaine Tyler. 2008. *Homeward Bound: American Families in the Cold War Era*. New York: Basic Books.

McAdams, Dan. P. 2001. "The Psychology of Life Stories." *Review of General Psychology* 5:2 (June): 100-22.

McAllister, Matthew P. and J. Mitt Giglio. 2005. "The Commodity Flow of U. S. Children's Television." *Critical Studies in Media Communication* 22:1 (March): 26-44.

McGhee, Paul E. 1972. "On the Cognitive Origins of Incongruity Humor." In *The Psychology of Humor*, edited by Jeffrey H. Goldstein and Paul E. McGhee, 61-80. New York: Academic Press.

Minkoff, David. 2010. *Oy! The Ultimate Book of Jewish Jokes*. New York: Barnes & Noble, Inc.

Morris, Aldon D. 1984. *The Origins of the Civil Rights Movement*. New York: The Free Press.

Murray, Susan. 2005. *Hitch Your Antenna to the Stars: Early Television and Broadcast Stardom*. New York: Routledge.

Nachman, Gerald. 2003. *Seriously Funny: The Rebel Comedians of the 1950s and 1960s*. New York: Pantheon.

Nadel, Alan. 2005. *Television in Black-and-White: Race and National Identity*. Lawrence: University of Kansas Press.

Neely, Michelle N. *et. al.* 2012. "Neural Correlates of Humor Detections and Appreciation in Children." *The Journal of Neuroscience* 32:5 (February): 1784-90.

Nesteroff, Klipf. 2015. *The Comedians*. New York: Grove Press.

Newkirk, Vann R. 2008. *Lynching in North Carolina: A History, 1865-1941*. Jefferson, NC: McFarland & Co.

Newman, David and Robert Benton. 1965. "Love in the Afternoon." New York *Herald Tribune*, January 24, 1965: 7-10 and 50.

O'Connell, Kathy. 2008. "Soupy Sales: Creating Local Television in the 1950s." Unpublished paper in author's possession.

Osgood, Dick. 1955. "Soupy Gets Network Show." *Detroit Free Press*, June 12, 1955: 50.

Osgood, Dick. 1981. *Wixie Wonderland: An Unauthorized 50-Year Diary of WXYZ Detroit*. Bowling Green, OH: Bowling Green University Popular Press.

Palmer, Jerry. 1994. *Taking Humor Seriously*. New York. Routledge.

Pecora, Norma, John P. Murray, and Ellen Ann Wartella. Eds. 2007. *Children and Television: Fifty Years of Research*. Mahwah, NJ: Lawrence Erlbaum.

Pintzuk, Edward. 1997. *Reds, Racial Justice, and Civil Liberties: Michigan Communists During the Cold War*. Minneapolis: MEP Publications.

Pizzolato, Nicola. 2013. *Challenging Global Capitalism: Labor, Migration, Radical Struggle and Urban Change in Detroit and Turin.* New York: Palgrave Macmillan.

Reidelbach, Maria. 1991. *Completely MAD: A History of the Comic Book and Magazine.* Boston: Little, Brown & Co.

Sachs, Oliver. 2017. *The River of Consciousness.* New York: Alfred A. Knopf.

Sales, Soupy (with Charles Salzberg). 2001. *Soupy Sez! My Zany Life and Times.* New York: M. Evans and Co., Inc.

Sales, Soupy. 2003. *Stop Me If You've Heard It!* New York: M. Evans and Co., Inc.

Schacter, Daniel L. *et. al.* 2011. "Memory Distortion: An Adaptive Strategy." *Trends in Cognitive Science* 15:10 (October): 467-74.

Schnider, Armin. 2018. *The Confabulating Mind: How the Brain Creates Reality*, second edition. New York: Oxford University Press.

Schrecker, Ellen. 1998. *Many Are the Crimes: McCarthyisms in America.* Boston: Little, Brown & Co.

Smith, Suzanne E. 1999. *Dancing in the Street: Motown and the Cultural Politics of Detroit.* Cambridge, MA: Harvard University Press.

Spigel, Lynn. 1992. *Make Room for TV: Television and the Family Ideal in Postwar America.* Chicago: The University of Chicago Press.

Stryker, Mark. 2019. *Jazz From Detroit.* Ann Arbor: University of Michigan Press.

Sugrue, Thomas J. 2005. *The Origins of the Urban Crisis: Race and Inequality in Postwar Detroit.* Princeton, NJ: Princeton University Press.

Talbert, Bob. 1979. "Soupy Sales Still No. 1 to Many of Us." *Detroit Free Press,* June 8, 1979: 55.

Teegarden, Carol. 1994. "Soupy DuJour." *Detroit Free Press*, September 28, 1994: 6C.

Thompson, Heather Ann. 2017. *Whose Detroit? Politics, Labor and Race in a Modern American City.* Ithaca, NY: Cornell University Press.

Tullock, John. 2000. *Watching Television Audiences.* New York: Oxford University Press.

Turner, Graeme. 2004. *Understanding Celebrity.* London: Sage.

Ward, Stephen. 2016. *In Love and Struggle: The Revolutionary Lives of James and Grace Lee Boggs.* Chapel Hill: University of North Carolina Press.

Watts, Stephen. 1997. *The Magic Kingdom: Walt Disney and the American Way of Life.* New York: Houghton Mifflin.

Wisse, Ruth R. 2013. *No Joke: Making Jewish Humor.* Princeton, NJ: Princeton University Press.

Yaroch, Patricia. 1958. "Family Knows '*Soupy's On.*'" *Detroit News,* May 12, 1958:20.